Reincarnation
vs.
Resurrection

Reincarnation vs. Resurrection

by
John Snyder

MOODY PRESS
CHICAGO

Except where indicated otherwise, all Scripture quotations in this book are from the *New American Standard Bible,* ©1960, 1962, 1963, 1968, 1971, 1972, 1973, 1975, and 1977 by The Lockman Foundation, and are used by permission.

The use of selected references from various versions of the Bible in this publication does not necessarily imply publisher endorsement of the versions in their entirety.

I am indebted to Dr. James Bjornstad, Dr. Lincoln Hurst, and Col. Samuel Milton for their valuable remarks and suggestions in the preparation of this manuscript.

Special thanks and appreciation go to my wife, Shirin, without whose unflagging energy in researching and typing, this project would have remained only a good intention.

Library of Congress Cataloging in Publication Data

Snyder, John, 1946-
    Reincarnation vs. resurrection.

    1. Reincarnation—Controversial literature.
2. Resurrection. I. Title.
BL515.S64   1984   129   83-23811
ISBN 0-8024-0321-2

1 2 3 4 5 6 7 Printing/AK/Year 89 88 87 86 85 84

Printed in the United States of America

Dedicated with love and
appreciation to my parents

Contents

Preface

The ancient Greeks told the story of a great monster called the Sphinx, which sat outside the city of Thebes. To everyone who passed by she put a riddle: What creature has two feet, three feet, and four feet, and is weakest when it has the most feet? She destroyed everyone who failed to solve the riddle, until Oedipus finally came up with the right answer: it is man, who crawls on all fours as an infant, then walks upright on two feet, and in old age moves only with the aid of a stick.

The issue of life after death brings us face to face with the riddle that surpasses all others. If we fail to solve it, like the Sphinx it promises to destroy us.

Over the centuries, only a handful of possible solutions to the riddle have been put forward. We are witnessing in our day the revival of one, the theory of reincarnation. This book will critically evaluate that theory, and give what I believe to be the only rational solution to the riddle of life after death.

I became interested in the issue of reincarnation while researching for an Easter debate on the topic "Reincarnation vs. Resurrection." In preparation, I entered into dialogue with believers in reincarnation and discovered that, for the most part, the general public does not have a good basic understanding of reincarnation.

When I raised the issue of reincarnation as opposed to resurrection, the response was often a quizzical, "Is there a difference?" In the minds of many people, any possible difference between the two is so slight that debating them is merely splitting hairs. Clearly, we need more careful and precise definitions of terms. The meanings of *resurrection* and *reincarnation* are not self-evident; and therefore it will require some effort to mark out the differences between them.

If we were only discussing a difference in the mechanics of human survival beyond death, then we would not be likely to gain the attention of many people. But as I shall attempt to show, the difference between reincarnation and resurrection can be understood correctly only when both ideas are viewed as representatives of two radically opposing philosophies—for neither resurrection nor reincarnation can exist independently of the world views of which they are a part.

The abundance of evidence for reincarnation is initially surprising; and in some cases, it even seems quite persuasive. However, this evidence becomes much less compelling when it starts to include psychic phenomena. Then it becomes clear that there are some rather subtle fallacies built into the theory of reincarnation, fallacies that are fundamental yet consistently overlooked by the vast majority of writers.

The reader of reincarnationist books and articles will undoubtedly be impressed with their "Who's Who" list of believers. This purportedly includes such people as: Pythagoras, Pindar, Socrates, Plato, Jesus, Paul the apostle, Origen, Shakespeare, Napoleon, Richard Wagner, Arthur Conan Doyle, Jack London, Thomas Carlyle, Victor Hugo, Ralph Waldo Emerson, Walt Whitman, Alfred Lord Tennyson, Charles Dickens, Leo Tolstoy, Sigmund Freud, Henry Ford, Charles A. Lindberg, and many others.[1]

But with little effort, this list may be shortened measurably. Jesus beyond question was not a teacher of reincarnation. The early church Father Origen spoke of some form of preexistence, but in no way evidenced a personal belief in repeated incarnations in a variety

1. Joseph Head and S.L. Cranston, *Reincarnation: The Phoenix Fire Mystery* (New York: Warner Books, 1977).

of human bodies. The reader in English can simply go directly to the primary sources and trim further.

Nevertheless, there will still remain an astonishing lineup of history's thinkers and doers who were firm believers in past lives. For many people today, this is enough to substantiate the theory of reincarnation. Whether or not such confidence can be supported by hard fact is a question to be considered in this book.

Subjectivism is always a temptation in any discussion of ultimate matters; and the life after death debate is no exception. Many believe that "religious questions" can be resolved simply by sincerity and strong feelings; believers of all faiths can fall prey to this notion.

Insofar as it is possible, I will avoid ad hominem arguments, since nothing is accomplished by attacking the ideas of others on the basis of anything except evidence and rational argument. It is folly to think that anyone will be persuaded or compelled by impugning someone's intelligence, education, or honesty.

Similarly, it is of no value for us to appeal to such imaginary things as "common sense," or "what everybody knows," nor to suggest that one belief is more or less weird or silly than another. In a universe where nearly anything is possible, it makes no sense to assume that either resurrection or reincarnation is more or less likely than the other, since we have no agreed-upon standard of probability. Apart from hard evidence brought forward in support of either position, neither view is intrinsically more probable than the other.

The least reliable, but perhaps most popular, criterion for evaluating the arguments is that of personal preference. However, what sounds nicer, is most comfortable, or appeals to one's tastes and sensibilities has only minimal relevance to the question. Whatever the universe turns out to be like, it seems unlikely that anyone's tastes or feelings will have much of an impact upon it. It is the assumption of this book that, whatever we *want* to believe, we are stuck with what *is*; and that our basic task is not to create belief systems and religions, but to discover if we can the actual shape of this world and the next.

My motive in writing this book is not negative. It is not my purpose to demolish someone's hope in one form of survival by arguing for another form; but rather to describe the solid hope of resurrection.

Finally, this book is not for those who have despaired of this life and are simply marking time until the next; it is not for those who hate this life; but for those who, despite adversity, love it and are seeking an understanding of it. For one's view of life after death determines the quality of one's present life.

Introduction

From academic symposia on life after death, to para-psychological research and past life therapy practices, to the popular level of "come-as-you-were" parties in California, indications are that belief in reincarnation may soon become the most commonly accepted theory of afterlife in America. For centuries, it has been the belief of the majority of the human race; now, according to some polls, it is accepted by at least one-fourth of all Americans. Not surprisingly, an even higher percentage of our college students embrace the idea.[1]

It appears that reincarnation's popularity among today's youth is not the result of any compelling arguments on its behalf, or because the theory offers fresh insights into the human condition, but simply because it is the most recent wind to blow across the land. In the absence of any substantial intellectual consensus to resist its force, it has come to occupy the atmosphere. It is a fashionable idea simply because of its novelty. No battle was fought and won, no revolution struggled for, no new invention made; nor were any of history's usual methods of radical change used. Instead, a vacuum was created

1. George Gallup, Jr., and William Procter, *Adventures in Immortality* (New York: McGraw-Hill, 1982), pp.137-38.

around us; and the air, already charged with Eastern philosophy, was quietly drawn in.

One attraction of reincarnation for our culture is its apparent belief in the eternal importance of people. At a time when belief in any form of life after death has been displaced by materialism, and when there has been a general loss of meaning in human life, belief in reincarnation offers some measure of hope. Those who have despaired of this life will grasp any straw of hope for another chance in some future life. When people see their loved ones slip away into an unknown void they may cling to any doctrine that seems to offer hope of a return. Most people long for some form of immortality, and reincarnation theory makes a direct appeal to this felt need.

But another reason for its warm reception is that it is very convenient to believe in reincarnation. It is easier to face than the prospect of giving account to an infinite, personal God who has the power to cast people into eternal separation. It appeals to the tastes and sensibilities of modern thinkers who prefer to believe that doctrines about God and humanity are unimportant, and that one way of life and belief is just as good an any other; it dovetails with the pervasive notion that all roads in a pluralistic society lead to the same end. For this convenient system predicts nothing less than the ultimate salvation of the human race.

Further, reincarnation appeals to human pride by teaching that one's final destiny is determined by one's own works and efforts, not by the actions of a supreme being. This view is especially alluring to our sinful natures. Most people who casually believe in reincarnation have not carefully thought through the rigorous program of discipline and effort implied in this teaching. Nevertheless, it is integral to belief in reincarnation.

Clearly, one of the reasons many opt for reincarnation theory is their abhorrence of the idea of personal guilt and responsibility. They see guilt as a harmful, fear-based emotion designed by unscrupulous people who want to control others. For reincarnationists, the solution to the guilt problem is to deny its validity and to regard all past experience—including adultery, cheating, lying, and cruelty—not as sins for which one is accountable before a personal

God, but rather as learning experiences, potential steps in one's upward development.

 Whatever the full reasons for the major shift in American thinking about survival after death, reincarnation is an idea whose time has come. In this present state of affairs it is important to suggest to thinking people why the theory of reincarnation is not the most reasonable option. The pages that follow shall attempt to show three things:

1. The case for reincarnation that has received a hearing among many intellectuals as well as lay people is based upon a fallacy so subtly smuggled into the evidence that it can easily go undetected.
2. The biblical view of resurrection is antithetical to, and forever incompatible with, the theory of reincarnation. All attempts to find reincarnation in the Bible must end in failure.
3. Resurrection as taught by Jesus of Nazareth is the only view of life after death that can stand up under critical fire.

Reincarnation

1
What Is Reincarnation?

Reincarnation has from antiquity been a widely accepted doctrine among Hindus and Buddhists. But it was also not uncommon to find it among a number of Greek philosophers, who termed it *metempsychosis*—literally, "change of souls." And even a handful of heretical Jews and Christians have held to reincarnation.

The belief as it is usually understood in Hinduism states that all life is essentially one: that plant, animal, and human life are so interrelated that souls are capable of "transmigrating" from one form of life to another. A person could have been an animal, plant, or mineral in some previous existence. However, this version is unpalatable to American tastes, and so the movement of human souls is in the newer version limited to human bodies. When discussing reincarnation in this book, I will be referring to this American version, which speaks only of previous lives in human form.[1]

In most of the popular literature, reincarnation is confused with "preexistence"; nowhere is the problem of definition more obvious than here. It is common to find representatives of the church from several ages propounding ideas that sound like reincarnation.

---

1. Students of Hinduism may find points of disagreement with my presentation of reincarnation teaching. This is due to the peculiar hybrid form which the doctrine has taken in Western cultures.

But they were almost always speaking of preexistence instead.

In simple terms, preexistence means that one can live in some form before entering the physical body. Naturally, those who believe in reincarnation also believe in preexistence; but those who believe in spiritual preexistence do not necessarily believe in reincarnation. A person can believe that he or she existed as a spirit before birth, while still believing in a single *bodily* existence. Some of the early church Fathers, as well as a few Jewish rabbis, held to spiritual preexistence, a doctrine that was routinely condemned by various church councils. But it is a historical and philosophical error to read belief in the full-blown doctrine of reincarnation into this.

For our purposes, then, reincarnation is the consecutive movement of the soul from one bodily, human life to another for the purpose of working its way back to its original home, oneness with the universe—a point at which all incarnation ceases and all bodily and material existence is a thing of the past.

I will now comment briefly upon some of the major elements of popular reincarnation theory.

Karma

One of the principle components of the theory of reincarnation is *karma*, the doctrine that everyone gets what he deserves. This idea is one of the most fascinating and startling aspects of the entire theory. While reading the literature, one is impressed by the certainty with which it is discussed and by the dominating role that it plays.

Stated simply, karma means that there is some force in the universe that causes every human on earth to build up credits or debits through his behavior. A person shapes the quality of his life in the next incarnation through his actions in this incarnation. If he commits evil in this life, then retribution may be expected in the next; whereas performing good in this life will assure him a place in the sun in the next. In this manner, most of life's mysteries and inequities can be accounted for: the suffering of children, mental illness, poverty, disasters of nature—all are the result of evil committed in past lives.

It is not surprising that millions of people prefer the doctrine of karma to other possibilities. The theory has many advantages. It may be applied to almost any problem and produce an explanation. The impersonal reign of karma metes out justice dispassionately; one may rest in the confidence that no evil will go unpunished and no good will be unrewarded.

But to the question "Who is the administrator of this highly sophisticated procedure of reward and punishment?" the answer must be a remarkable, "No one"! There is no administrator per se, no infinite, personal God who oversees creation, but some impersonal process that in some remarkable way dispenses something akin to justice with all the efficiency of a computer, never making the mistake of punishing or rewarding the wrong person. What analogies do we have in this life to suggest that such a thing could be a reality? There is frightfully little in our experience that would encourage us to believe in such a force.

Another question arises: How does one discover the requirements of karma? In India, the belief in karma has the companion doctrine of the caste system, which to some extent provides direction as to the kind of behavior that is expected; but in the Western version there appears to be no way of knowing what karma really enjoins us to do. In actual practice, then, this allows each person to determine for himself what is good and evil.

This naturally places the onus of salvation entirely upon the individual, who by his own will and preference determines the course and values of his life. Such a theory fits hand-in-glove into the contemporary outlook. However, this freedom to arbitrarily choose standards contains the seeds of its own undoing; and its initial attractiveness peels away under the first hot blast of criticism.

How could anyone validate his standard of right and wrong? And how does one link up his own set of values with those of others to make the system work? Surely, the standards of National Socialism, which led to the mass destruction of Jews, could not qualify as good. Or consider the religion of Shinto, which through the Kamikazees elevated suicide to an act of worship. On what basis could it be said that either of those was not good or right, and of karmic value in securing future status in the next incarnation? Books could be filled with examples of religious slaughters, cultic mass murders, human sacrifices, and heretic-killings; all show that no absolute standard can be raised without an infinite, personal God to sustain it. Ironically, abilities affirmed for an impersonal force by reincarnationists are elsewhere denied to a personal Creator.

The difficulty in reaching a standard of behavior for the human family is intensified by the reincarnationist's presumption that once we had found such a standard, somehow we would have the strength to observe it. If the history of religion tells us anything, it is that even the best intentions do not provide people with the power to do what they think right. Jews with their law, Muslims with their ethics, Christians with their mores and morality all find that there is something in us that prevents us from attaining moral excellence. Even on the mundane level, how many times have we promised ourselves that we would start reading one book per week, or would rise up early in the morning and exercise, or join a club and make new friends, and it simply did not get done? If we cannot fulfill our aspirations on this elementary level, how can we hope to attain anything on the moral level?

In the final analysis then, karma is not the benevolent distributor of justice that we had thought, but is rather a malignant force that turns on us and becomes a cruel taskmaster. Human experience suggests that the buildup of karmic debt is so great as to be unpayable. To think otherwise leads to another problem with the theory of reincarnation, its view of the human spirit.

The Essential Goodness of the Human Spirit

Almost without exception, popularizers of reincarnation hold that man is fundamentally good and capable of doing right. This view is virtually the same as that of the Renaissance and of those ancient Greeks who believed that people, understood from the point of view of their rational capacities, are basically on the right track; that momentary departures were the result not of some profound moral flaw in the center of the human spirit, but rather of ignorance; and that if people just could be shown the truth, they would naturally follow after it.[2]

2. Reinhold Niebuhr, *The Nature and Destiny of Man*, vol. 1 (New York: Scribner's, 1964), pp. 4-18.

Such notions, then as now, lead to unbounded optimism. Reincarnationists see the future of the human race as a gradual—but certain—ascent. Such a view is maintained not on the basis of evidence; rather it is a philosophical a priori, never a point to be proved but an axiom to to be accepted.

Here the controlling principle is humanism rather than Hinduism; and this can be seen even more clearly in the next component of reincarnation theory.

Evolution

The modus operandi of classical Hinduism is the movement, or transmigration, of souls from one body to another, occurring in either direction: The soul can progress spiritually upward into another human body, or downward into animal, plant, or mineral bodies, depending upon its karma. However, this point of view is almost always repudiated by Western reincarnationists because it seems too crude, and because the suggestion of a downward slide is unpalatable to modern tastes. To relieve contemporary anxieties, aspects of evolutionary theory are imported to supply the power for the desired ascent of humanity.

Optimism

The ideological twin of evolutionary theory is unrestrained optimism. To be a reincarationist of the popular order, one must be willing to put aside every semblance of caution in order to see a bright future, a trademark of the modern mentality. Recent reincarnationist writers indicate that even the most base and malign characters in history are ultimately destined to ascend the scale toward enlightenment in some future incarnation. This rosy view of future prospects is entirely unrelated to human experience.

Monism

Although a handful of reincarnationist writers believe it possible to be a theistic reincarnationist, the philosophy that is most at home with—and indeed, which is the mother of—reincarnation, is Monism. In its simplest terms, Monism is the belief that ultimately everything in the universe is one; that is, that there can be no fundamental distinctions between human beings, animals, earth, or God. When everything is accounted for, they say, we are all only fragments or aspects of God, and our destiny is to be reunited with this Oneness.

This is the fundamental principle of Hinduism and its offshoots, and it is quickly detected when reincarnationists level their guns at the Christian doctrine of an infinite, personal God. Occasionally a writer indicates that he has nothing against the church or its teaching on most subjects, but this generally signals either a superficial understanding of what the church teaches or an outright rejection of the New Testament doctrine of God. When the veneer of friendliness is peeled away, a profound hostility to the biblical view of God is exposed, and in many cases there is no attempt to hide it. There can be no real peaceful coexistence between Monism and the Christian doctrine of God, for the views are forever incompatible.

Immortality of the Soul

The theory of reincarnation would be incoherent apart from the ancient doctrine of the immortality of the soul. It affirms that the potential for eternal life resides in the soul, which will inevitably live on with or without the body. In other words, the soul is believed to have eternal properties of its own that cannot be taken away.

This teaching is not, as many think, the view of the Bible or the teaching of Jesus. As widespread as it is, it cannot be supported from Scripture. For the Bible, the only source of life, either on this earth or in some other state of existence, is God, who gives life as a gift. There was a time when we did not exist in any form whatsoever, and it is perfectly within the realm of possibility for us not to exist at all if God so chooses it. Reincarnationists may insist upon the doctrine of the soul's immortality—in fact, the theory cannot exist without it—but the idea cannot claim biblical sanction.

The difference between the reincarnationist's view of the soul and the biblical view is that the former sees the soul continuing to live whether or not a personal, infinite God exists, simply because of its own immortal character, whereas the Bible indicates that a personality continues only to the extent that God grants it existence.

Although it is true that most resurrectionists believe that the immaterial aspect of a person continues after death to be reunited to a transformed body at the resurrection, the heart of this affirmation is not a doctrine of an independent soul, but the insistence that it is God alone who wills and grants life.

•   •   •

With the above serving as a working definition of reincarnation theory, it is possible now to consider the evidence for it.

2

Evidence for Reincarnation

Most popular literature on reincarnation is not very impressive, either in the strength of its evidence or in its care for detail. But there has been some cautious and exhaustive research that has uncovered a number of well-documented stories, adding weight to the case for reincarnation. The stories cited here are from Ian Stevenson's book *Twenty Cases Suggestive of Reincarnation*.[1]

Two Case Studies

In April 1950, a boy of ten named Nirmal died of smallpox in his parents' home in Kosi Kalan, a town in the District of Mathura, Uttar Pradesh in India. In August 1951 a son, Prakash, was born to the wife of Sri Brijlal Varshnay in the town of Chhatta.

At the age of about four-and-one-half Prakash began to tell his parents that he belonged in Kosi Kalan, six miles away. Claiming that his name was really Nirmal, he pleaded with his parents to take him back to his real home in Kosi Kalan. In 1961, the father and sister of the dead boy, Nirmal, passed through the town of Chhatta on a business trip; having heard of Prakash and his claims, they visited him. Prakash immediately recognized them as his father and sister

---

1. Ian Stevenson, *Twenty Cases Suggestive of Reincarnation* (New York: American Society for Psychical Research, 1966), pp. 20-33, 246-79.

from his previous life. Soon after, when he actually visited the home in Kosi Kalan, he was able to recognize other members of Nirmal's family, as well as places in the home. Not surprisingly, Nirmal's parents became convinced that their dead son had been reborn as Prakash.

Imad Elawar was born on December 21, 1958, in Kornayel, a village 15 miles east of Beirut, Lebanon. When Imad was less than two years old, he began to talk about his previous life. As he became more articulate, he claimed to have lived in the village of Khriby (20 miles southeast of Beirut) with the Bouhamzy family, and mentioned a number of people and events familiar to him, as well as property he owned as a member of the Bouhamzy clan.

In December 1963, Imad's father and uncle traveled to Khriby to attend the funeral of a prominent official of Khriby, Mr. Said Bouhamzy, a member of the family to which Imad claimed to have belonged in his previous life. At the funeral two of the names given by Imad were confirmed, and the family began to think that perhaps Imad was telling the truth.

Imad's remarks became more and more startling and specific. Frequently he would refer to a woman named Jamile and to his happiness at being able to walk—as if he had been lame in the past. So confidently did he say these things that the family began researching the matter. Soon it was discovered that in the village of Khriby there had lived a man by the name of Ibrahim Bouhamzy, that he had had a beautiful mistress named Jamile, and that he had died of spinal tuberculosis on September 18, 1949. The disease, causing him great difficulty in walking, had rendered him bedridden for the last two months of his life.

When Imad was eventually brought by his parents to Ibrahim's house for formal introductions, he demonstrated clear recognition of family members and various objects in the home. Traits common to Imad and Ibrahim were discovered: their fondness for a certain kind of tea and their remarkable facility with the French language (which greatly impressed the family, since Ibrahim had learned fluent French while serving in the French army). During this visit many other points of contact between the two personalities were established. This was enough for Imad's family; they were persuaded that their son had, indeed, lived before as Ibrahim.

There is an impressive number of similar reports of children and adults who "remember" places, people, and events that could not have been known to them under normal circumstances. To an increasing number of people, this evidence seems at least initially compelling.

The reasons for this appeal are not difficult to understand. First, the theory is attractive because it is a novelty, out of the ordinary for most Westerners. Second, it offers a ready explanation for phenomena that are inexplicable by any conventional theory. And finally, it is well known that a striking number of the world's leaders and thinkers, from ancient to contemporary times, were believers in reincarnation—not to mention the growing lineup of noted personalities who appear in the media discussing their newly found selves.

The honest inquirer, however, will want to consider *all* the evidence at hand, as well as the reasonable alternatives to the theory. In fact, the view is vulnerable when subjected to any kind of logical critique.

Retrocognition and Reincarnation

In virtually all reincarnationist literature, there is one rarely questioned assumption: that *cognition implies presence*. It is assumed that if someone has unexplained, detailed knowledge of persons, places, or things in the past, it must follow that he or she was actually there in some form: in other words, if I remember a past life, then it has to be *my* life that I remember.

But must this be so? The entire superstructure of reincarnation theory stands or falls on the way in which cases of retrocognition (knowledge of the past) are manipulated into "proof" for the reality of past lives. If it could be shown beyond doubt that some of the best examples of retrocognition are cases where reincarnation is *impossible*, then it would not be necessary to look to reincarnation for an explanation. And in fact, it will become apparent as we continue that the inference of past lives from the data of retrocognition is simply another example of that age-old fallacy, non sequitur—"it does not follow."

Some of the best examples of retrocognition actually *exclude* possibility of reincarnation. Such a case is that of Peter Hurkos.[2]

Peter Hurkos

Born Pieter van der Hurk in Holland in May of 1911, Hurkos was working as a house painter during World War II when he fell from a building and sustained a severe head injury. While convalescing in the Zuidwal Hospital in The Hague, a mysterious knowledge came to him. He writes in the opening pages of his autobiography:

> After the nurse had gone I noticed another man in the bed next to mine. I had never seen this man before, but suddenly I knew a great deal about him—without either one of us having said a word.
>
> "You're a bad man," I blurted out.
>
> He looked at me, startled, not knowing whether to be annoyed or amused at a poor joke.
>
> "Why?" he asked.
>
> "Because when your father died, he left you a large gold watch—he died only a short time ago, and you have already sold the watch."
>
> The man in the next bed was dumbfounded. "How did you know that?" he asked, turning toward me.
>
> I felt my head. How had I known it? I was as dumbfounded as he was.[3]

Hurkos detected that another patient was a secret agent working for the British, and that he would be killed soon. Shortly afterward, when he read the confirmation of this in the newspaper, his life was changed. He set about his life's work, which stands as one of the most celebrated and astounding examples of retrocognition in modern history. Hurkos was accurate in his knowledge of past things, events, and people a startling 87-99 percent of the time!

The *form* of his knowledge is strikingly similar to that of the "memories" that supposedly point to reincarnation. We understand true memory to be both *particular* and *sequential*. *Particular*, in that it contains details both relevant and irrelevant, important and trivial;

2. Norma Lee Browning, *The Psychic World of Peter Hurkos* (Garden City, N.Y.: Doubleday, 1970); Peter Hurkos, *Psychic* (Indianapolis: Bobbs-Merrill, 1961); Andrija Puharich, *Beyond Telepathy* (Garden City, N.Y.: Doubleday, 1962).

often one's memory retains the inconsequential and completely leaves out the significant. (We forget Uncle Charlie's advice, but we remember that he was wearing a green hat when he gave it.) Memory is also *sequential*, in that events are often remembered in the order in which they occurred. In bolstering their case, reincarnationists point to instances of retrocognition that display these characteristics of true memory. But one is impressed by exactly the same kind of knowledge in Hurkos.

And this knowledge is found in Hurkos with a degree of precision found only occasionally in the evidence for reincarnation. In the case of the stolen Stone of Scone (the royal coronation stone in Westminster Abbey), Hurkos possessed accurate knowledge of the scene of the theft, the route taken by the thieves (including the street names, correctly spelled), the final destination of the stone, the motives for the theft, the time of its return, and even some personal details about the thieves. He gave the same sort of information to a search party looking for a small plane that had gone down in the rugged mountains of California, to the police in the search for the Boston Strangler, and in many other cases.

The cognition exhibited by Hurkos is similar to that which is most often cited as evidence by reincarnationists; yet the knowledge he possessed was usually about people, places, and things that existed *after his birth*. Even more telling, he was capable of "remembering" intimate details of the lives of two or more persons who lived simultaneously.[4] No one could possibly argue that he obtained his information during a previous life.

As we have seen, reincarnationists argue that cognition indicates presence—that is, "I could not know it unless I was there." But surely this argument is falsified by considering *all* the evidence. No one would argue that Peter Hurkos acquired his knowledge of the past by his personal presence. Even his knowledge of events that occurred before his birth does not suggest that Hurkos was present when the events occurred. He merely knew about them.

Reincarnationists do not themselves dispute the psychic abilities of Peter Hurkos. They simply have not considered the great

4. Ibid.

problems which he poses for their theory. And psychic research provides us with a great number of similarly documented cases, where people have experienced cognition of events and people in the distant past, the recent past, the present, and the future. In these instances reincarnation is the least plausible explanation.

This study of psychic history is not for the purpose of placing an imprimatur upon belief in psychic phenomena, but rather to show that reincarnation theory is internally incoherent. Even the doubtful evidence that reincarnationists muster does not finally validate their case.

Psychic Knowledge and Reincarnation

It is easy to anticipate the objection of reincarnationists at this point: Peter Hurkos's retrocognition, they will say, is not of the same type as past-life memory—it is only psychic knowledge. But this objection carries little weight since it begs the question, assuming that which is to be proved. Surely we have no way of knowing that they are different types unless we already know that reincarnation is true—the very thing to be demonstrated!

We cannot piggyback one logical fallacy upon another to prove a theory, nor can we combine our relative ignorance of the psychic world with our ignorance of life after death and hope to come up with accurate classifications of psychic knowledge. Reincarnationists throw caution to the wind when they use the word *memory* to describe retrocognition; and the unwary reader can easily get drawn in. Retrocognition can legitimately be called memory only *after* reincarnation is proved.

It may still appear that there are two different types of retrocognition—that of Hurkos and that of Nirmal and Imad. But someone experiencing retrocognition for the first time—especially a child—would quite naturally regard this information as memory, since that is the most common explanation of such mental images. Even if Nirmal or Imad had been born in a Western country where belief in reincarnation was not common, their experiences would still seem like memories to them. Much the same is true even in cases of adult retrocognition. While the assumption of memory is a natural one, it is not necessarily legitimate. These "memories," taken by themselves, remain facts in search of a theory; and reincarnation is only one of a number of possible interpretations. Belief in reincarnation is never simply a *conclusion* based on facts; it is first and foremost a *decision* of faith.

Ian Stevenson argues that reincarnation is generally more likely when the subject's retrocognition focuses on the memories of a single past life, whereas psychic knowledge tends to be about a number of lives.[5] The cases cited in chapter one, compared with the example of Peter Hurkos, show that distinction quite well.

But for every instance that supports reincarnation in that way, there is another that raises serious doubts. Reincarnation researcher Brad Steiger describes a case considered by the Rev. Leslie Weatherhead to be suggestive of reincarnation.[6]

While on a tour of an excavated Roman villa on the outskirts of Naples with his mother and a noted archaeologist, David became very excited upon reaching the site. He ran to and fro until he came to a Roman bath engraved with the signs of the Zodiac. Here he began recalling memories of his past lives.

In another excursion, David and his parents were visiting a cave in Guernsey, a channel island of England. Tapping the walls, he claimed that there was yet another cave, where a young prisoner had been walled in, and that he had in another life watched it being done. Authorities denied that such a cave existed, but upon further investigation discovered that David had indeed been right and that the name he had given for the dead prisoner corresponded with the name in the archives.

When David was fourteen, he went with his mother to see some newly acquired mummies at the British Museum. After peering inside a sarcophagus, he complained that there should have been three initials on the underside of the case. He claimed that he possessed such knowledge because he had been an inspector of those very coffins in some previous life.

This story is significant for two reasons. First, here is a case that would meet Stevenson's evidential criterion, in that the focus of

5. Stevenson, pp. 332-33; 339.
6. Brad Steiger, *You Will Live Again* (New York: Dell, 1978).

retrocognition is on one life at a time (i.e., the "memories" are like those that a single individual would have). But the idea that this is a true case of reincarnation seems farfetched even to reincarnationists such as Brad Steiger. Second, David's capacities for retrocognition are strikingly similar to those of Peter Hurkos. Reincarnationists resent giving ground to psychic phenomena as an explanation for retrocognition, but there is painfully little that *cannot* be accounted for by such psychic phenomena.

This critique is not dependent upon the stories of Peter Hurkos and David; many other examples could be drawn upon. And more importantly, the case for reincarnation falls down in the way it logically manipulates the phenomenon of retrocognition— not just in the number of particular instances of retrocognition.

To sum up: retrocognition, to the extent that psychic research proves it true, implies nothing more than a knowledge of the past. It in no way points to actual presence in the past. Only a leap of wishful thinking can bridge the great gulf that exists between the evidence for retrocognition and reincarnation theory. At present, psychic knowledge is not even partially understood or explained, but it is clear that whatever its nature, it cannot bear the evidential weight placed upon it by the enthusiastic proponents of reincarnation.

The Evidence of Birthmarks

Another datum used as evidence by reincarnationists is the appearance of birthmarks.[7] A rope burn on the neck could indicate that a person was hanged in some previous life; a series of what appear to be healed-over bullet wounds could mean a person was shot in another life. The reincarnationist argues that whereas conventional psychic knowledge might be an explanation for reincarnational "memories," they cannot explain instances in which birthmarks correspond to the wounds known to have been on the deceased person's body.

That might sound plausible upon first hearing, but it can carry no more weight than the argument from retrocognition. For those birthmarks are equally as mysterious to the reincarnationist as

7. Stevenson, pp. 79-93, 134-50, 231-40, 348-49.

to his critic. To use this argument to advantage, it would first have to be shown that there is some known mechanism that enables a reincarnated personality to reproduce physical scars on the new body. But no such mechanism is known. Even if reincarnation already were a proved fact, we would still have no information as to *how* the personality could impose upon its new physical home the marks of the earlier one.

Psychic history, as well as medical history and research into the area of the demonic, suggest to us that mind and body are so linked as to be able to produce on the physical dimension virtually any type of mark or reaction that the spirit—or spirits—may determine.

Therefore, in principle, these birthmarks *might* be construed as corroborative evidence for reincarnation—if the theory held up on other grounds—but they just as easily qualify as physical manifestations of psychic retrocognition or demonic activity. This evidence possesses a rather *neutral* quality.

The psychic explanation has been introduced to suggest one alternative explanation (in my view a more consistent and reasonable one) to belief in reincarnation. Yet this is not the only alternative. Careful researchers have offered several other possibilities not inconsistent with the facts, which are discussed in the next chapter.

3
Other Explanations

A few reincarnationist writers suggest alternate ways to interpret evidence suggestive of reincarnation. No one exercises more caution or care for detail in sifting through the data than Ian Stevenson in his book *Twenty Cases Suggestive of Reincarnation.* He offers five alternate explanations for the evidence.[1]

(1) *Fraud.* An outright, conscious attempt to fool others is a likely explanation in many alleged cases of reincarnation. But it is probably the least likely alternative in many of the more closely studied cases. No doubt fraud exists, but in Stevenson's and my view it is an inadequate explanation for the more sophisticated evidence.

(2) *Cryptomnesia.* This is the condition in which someone knows about a person but later forgets the source of this information and in time so identifies with the deceased person that he genuinely feels he *is* the other. Again, this explanation may be the best for some cases, but it runs out of steam when faced with a situation in which no known source of information for the deceased person exists or when the personal identification is so intense that it carries throughout the influenced person's lifetime.

1. Stevenson, *Twenty Cases Suggestive of Reincarnation* (New York: American Society for Psychical Research, 1966), pp. 291-315.

(3) *Genetic "Memory."* This hypothesis suggests that through the physical lineage of generations, memory can be transmitted through the genetic structure in approximately the same way that instinct allows a bird to fly to its "home" far from the place where it was hatched. The obvious problem with this view is that, whereas it may make sense in the case of a direct descendant of the personality presumed to be reincarnated—and even in cases in which several generations stand between subjects—it does not explain "memories" of people who are not related to those they remember.

(4) *Extrasensory Perception Plus Personation.* Personation, the sort of close identification with another that we saw displayed in cryptomnesia, fails to account for richer examples of retrocognition. But when extrasensory perception (ESP) is added to the mix, much more may be explained. However, the extent to which ESP or psychic knowledge accounts for the evidences is, as we have seen, a fundamental disagreement between reincarnationists and their opponents.

(5) *Possession.* Another option frequently favored by reincarnationists is spirit possession. Due to the great consequences that follow from this admission, a more detailed response shall be devoted to this hypothesis.

Spirit Possession

Stevenson supplies us with a working definition of possession as distinct from reincarnation. Possession is the entering of a discarnate personality into another person's body, sometime after embryonic development, whereas when a personality enters a body at conception or during the development of the embryo it is regarded as reincarnation. In the former instance, the primary or original personality gives way, in varying degrees, to the influencing or secondary personality; in the latter instance, the original personality is the only one present.

I will give two examples of possession. First, the Gifford-Thompson case[2]: Thompson, an engraver with little skill or interest in painting, one day felt a nearly irresistible compulsion to paint. As

2. Ibid., pp. 340-47.

he yielded to the desire, he produced with unusual skill scenes on canvas that strongly resembled the favorite or often frequented places of Robert Swain Gifford, a well-known painter who had died six months before. Thompson had known Gifford slightly during his life, but had not heard of his death.

A careful examination of the data by researchers seems to indicate that Thompson fell under the influence of Gifford's personality. Frequently, Thompson would tell his wife that Gifford wanted to go sketching in this place or that, and he would travel to some of Gifford's favorite places in the country to paint or sketch. Sometimes the impressions would be accompanied by voices urging Thompson on, as well as hallucinations of scenes that would "demand" to be painted. Sometimes Thompson would experience amnesia as to certain works that he had produced under the influence of Gifford. In no case did Thompson ever indicate that he thought himself to be Gifford. There was always a clear distinction in his mind between himself and the personality of the deceased painter.

A second case of apparent possession is that of Lurancy Vennum.[3] She was seemingly possessed by a personality named Mary Roff, who had died when Lurancy was one year old. For a period of three months, Mary Roff apparently took over the body of Lurancy Vennum to such an extent that only Mary's personality remained. At the end of three months, Mary Roff disappeared and Lurancy returned. The displacement recurred intermittently afterwards, but at no time did Lurancy ever claim to be Mary or vice-versa. Moreover, Mary never seemed to be able to adapt to living as Lurancy Vennum.

What Kind of Spirits?

These cases of possession raise the question: Who is doing the possessing? According to Stevenson, discarnate personalities are either morally neutral or benign—the soul of a departed painter entering into another's body in order to do some afternoon sketching, the spirit of a deceased girl taking over another body for some unknown, seemingly harmless reason, and so forth.

Stevenson's reasoning can be faulted only in that it does not

3. Ibid., pp. 228-29, 341-46.

go far enough. As well as the possibility of possession by discarnate personalities who have departed this world, why not also consider the possibility of malignant spirits who have never had nor ever will have human bodies to call their own? The ancient world was not unfamiliar with such phemonena, as can be seen in some New Testament accounts (e.g., Matthew 8:30-34; Mark 8:32-34; Luke 4:31-37; Acts 16:16-18; 19:11-16).

Once the door has been opened to the possibility of possession by personalities from some other dimension—once we have flung wide the gateway of the nonmaterial world—then surely we cannot be overly particular as to what might come through it.

Some have suggested that the ultimate explanation of the evidence for past lives is demonic deception: that spiritual forces are working to deceive humans into believing in reincarnation.

The belief that the realm of the demonic plays a role in the evidence for reincarnation should not be quickly brushed aside. It is not uncommon for someone hearing this view to laugh scornfully and to dismiss the suggestion, never really considering the possibility seriously because it sounds like the last resort of the simple-minded. However, one should ponder this possibility for a moment.

Consider everyday human life. What do we know about it? When asked, "Is anyone trying to deceive us?" we reflect upon all that we know, and we must answer, "Yes." It does not take a great deal of investigation to conclude that there are powerful forces in the world which are trying to deceive most people much of the time. Governments deceive the populace about their clandestine activities; corporations deceive the public as to their secret intent; criminals deceive the police; landlords deceive their tenants, children their parents, parents their children, spouses each other, automobile companies their buyers, taxpayers the tax collector, employees their bosses; and we all even deceive ourselves. The list could go on ad infinitum.

Is there deception in the world? A person would be considered a simpleton to think otherwise.

In view of this, it cannot be unreasonable to ask whether there might be spirit beings who are busy trying to deceive us. Unless one is a pure materialist of the sort that denies the existence of all spiritual realities, the question must be significant. There is no reason in principle that there should not be as much deception on the spiritual level as there is on the natural, everyday level. Only the most incautious person would assume that deception could occur in the natural realm but never in the supernatural. The view that evil is present only in the physical dimension and that the spirit-dimension is free from evil is an ancient dualistic notion. This popular superstition seems to have an evergreen quality about it. A careful person should want to assume that if there is a spirit realm, then there is no good reason why there should not be as much deception by and of its inhabitants as there is among us earth-dwellers.

The question at this point is, What would motivate such forces to attempt to deceive the human race? This will be taken up in the final section of this book.

4
Out-of-the-Body Experiences

The growing professional and academic work in the area of death and dying has not been ignored by reincarnationists. Once studied predominantly from a psychological or medical point of view, research into the experience and stages of death has spawned full-blown investigations of "out-of-the-body" experiences. This research has been used as evidence that the traditional Christian notion of separate destinies after death is no longer feasible. And it is believed by many that such evidence points to reincarnation.

In a typical account,[1] a person who is legally dead (i.e., all his life support systems have apparently failed) returns to life with a report of what happened in the intervening period. It is common to hear that he or she left the body and was able to view the entire scene from somewhere above or around the deathbed, sometimes hearing the conversation of doctors or nurses, perhaps even traveling to other rooms and hearing conversations there. Other common ingredients of the experience include hearing buzzing and ringing, a sensation of moving at great speeds, and approaching an intense light. The subject generally feels himself welcomed after death by some benevolent force.

1. Raymond A. Moody, Jr., *Life After Life* (New York: Bantam Books, 1975), pp. 21ff.

These elements have appeared so frequently in the interviews of recovered patients that it has led investigators to take the question of life after death more seriously. Now a burgeoning field of scientific research, this study has attracted the attention of many specialists in psychology, parapsychology, and medicine. The results of the research are such that now it is probably not reasonable to be a thoroughgoing skeptic in these matters; yet one must retain a strong degree of caution until more extensive work has been done. Still, some things can be said about the pertinence of these out-of-the-body experiences as evidence for reincarnation.

It would seem that if one *does* accept the stories as true, then it would be reasonable to accept not only accounts of death's warm friendship, but also those reports that indicate the opposite. A substantial amount of evidence suggests that many who slip into this intermediate state have a decidedly *hellish* experience.[2]

It is not uncommon for a patient to move in and out between this world and some terrible state of alienation. In the cases of the warm, friendly experience, patients recall the event readily, but the patient who has had a nightmarish encounter tends to block it from his mind. This repression of the memory usually occurs immediately afterward—so that the patient does not even remember in the recovery room. The only ones to know of his experience are the doctors or friends who hear him while he is describing it.

So the evidence is mixed and is at best inconclusive as to whether death is a friend or an enemy, or whether the reception into the afterlife is a happy one or not.

As to the pertinence of this research to our purposes, it does not seem that it can be used to prove—or even to suggest— either reincarnation *or* resurrection; and it would not help to read into these stories more significance than there actually is. With this limitation in mind, however, a few things may be said:

1. The out-of-the-body experiences that have been reported, whether genuine or not, do not in themselves *teach* anything in particular. They may have some corroborative value in saying something about life after death, but they are open to a variety of

2. Maurice Rawlings, *Beyond Death's Door* (Nashville: Thomas Nelson, 1978).

interpretations, both metaphysical and psychological. Although they may indicate that there is some intermediate stage between this life and something else, they do not tell us what that something else is. Either resurrectionists or reincarnationists may reasonably adopt this evidence for their own purposes.

2. Out-of-the-body reports and their interpretations confront us with the question of authority. Eventually, we must ask: Who has the right to tell us about the nature of death and realities beyond it? Even if at some future time everyone who experienced out-of-the-body phenomena came to believe the same theory of afterlife, what would that say about the truth of that theory? Would we not be better off if we could base our opinion upon some solid authority rather than a consensus of opinion formed by personal experiences? But this question is somewhat premature and will be set out more clearly in the section entitled "The Case for Resurrection."

5

Reincarnation and the Bible

It is difficult to pick up any written work on reincarnation that does not see the Bible—particularly the teaching of Jesus—as an ally. Invariably, however, no attempt is made to apprehend this teaching within a broad and balanced perspective; rather, isolated and obscure texts are pressed into service in a purely artificial and perfunctory way. The following are the most commonly used passages to support the theory of reincarnation.

"Naked Shall I Return"

An Old Testament passage popular among reincarnationists is Job 1:20-21:

> Then Job arose and tore his robe and shaved his head, and he fell to the ground and worshiped. And he said, "Naked I came from my mother's womb, and naked I shall return there. The Lord gave and the Lord has taken away. Blessed be the name of the Lord."

This passage is of value to us for two reasons. First, although initially seeming friendly toward reincarnation, it actually works *against* the theory; and secondly, it shows us one of the first principles of biblical interpretation.

A cardinal rule for interpreting Scripture is that each passage must be understood in its original context. By *context* I mean not only the textual setting of ideas and phrases, but also the wider setting of ideas prevalent during the time of composition. This holds true, of course, for the interpretation not only of the Bible, but of any literature. If a person wants to find out what a passage means, he looks at surrounding phrases, sentences, and paragraphs. He also takes into account uses of metaphor, imagery, figures of speech, and so forth.

By itself, Job 1:21 gives the impression that at some future time one returns to one's mother's womb; reincarnationists see this as referring to another birth. But such an interpretation cannot be sustained. Even if the passage were understood in its most literal sense and without regard for context, it still would not suggest reincarnation, since rarely, according to reincarnationists, does anyone return to his own mother's womb.

The matter is cleared up further by seeing what the Old Testament writers meant when they referred to the *womb*. Genesis 3:19 shows that the Hebrews believed that man came from the dust of the *earth* when originally created by God, and to the dust (i.e., the earth) he shall return. The understanding of the womb as "the earth" is made, for example, in Psalm 139:13-15:

> For Thou didst form my inward parts;
> Thou didst weave me in my mother's womb.
> I will give thanks to Thee, for I am fearfully and wonderfully
>   made.
> Wonderful are Thy works,
> And my soul knows it very well.
> My frame was not hidden from Thee,
> When I was made in secret,
> And skillfully wrought in the depths of the earth.

Confirmation that the writer of Job also meant to use the imagery of the womb in this way can be found in Job 38: 8, 29.

So this passage says neither more nor less than what any Old Testament writer would say about the nature of life— that we are created from the elements of the earth by the hand of God, that we

come into this world naked and empty-handed, and that we shall
return to the earth through bodily decay.

"He Himself Is Elijah"

A central biblical text for many reincarnationists is Matthew
17:1-13:

And six days later Jesus took with Him Peter and James and John his
brother, and brought them up to a high mountain by themselves. And He
was transfigured before them; and His face shone like the sun, and His
garments became as white as light. And behold, Moses and Elijah
appeared to them, talking with Him. And Peter answered and said to
Jesus, "Lord, it is good for us to be here; if You wish, I will make three
tabernacles here, one for You, and one for Moses, and one for Elijah."
While he was still speaking, behold, a bright cloud overshadowed them;
and behold, a voice out of the cloud, saying, "This is My beloved Son,
with whom I am well-pleased; listen to Him!" And when the disciples
heard this, they fell on their faces and were much afraid. And Jesus came
to them and touched them and said, "Arise, and do not be afraid." And
lifting up their eyes, they saw no one, except Jesus Himself alone.
And as they were coming down from the mountain, Jesus
commanded them, saying, "Tell the vision to no one until the Son of
Man has risen from the dead." And His disciples asked Him, saying,
"Why then do the scribes say that Elijah must come first?" And He
answered and said, "Elijah is coming and will restore all things; but I
say to you, that Elijah already came, and they did not recognize him,
but did to him whatever they wished. So also the Son of Man is going to
suffer at their hands." Then the disciples understood that He had
spoken to them about John the Baptist.

The story of the transfiguration of Jesus, in which Moses and
Elijah appear with Him on the mountain, is understood by many to
mean that John the Baptist was the reincarnation of Elijah. Yet this
can make sense only if one neglects to examine both the related
passages and the general thought world of the New Testament. Such
a study will show that it is impossible for this passage to be teaching
reincarnation.

By the time the transfiguration of Jesus took place, John the
Baptist had already been killed by Herod. According to reincarna-

tion theory, then, John the Baptist and not Elijah should have appeared on the mountain, because the Baptist would have been the more recent incarnation.

More importantly, we find in 2 Kings 2:11 that Elijah was one of the few people in biblical history believed never to have seen death; thus, Elijah was simply not available for the recycling process. All the preliminary biblical data, therefore, does not support the idea that John the Baptist was an incarnation of Elijah.

Much has been made of this connection between Elijah and John the Baptist in reincarnationist literature. To read those books, one would think that it was the only thing Jesus ever said on the subjects of death and future life in three years of teaching. How much more plainly could reincarnation be taught, it is often said, than in the declaration in Matthew 11:14, "He himself is Elijah"?

But the painfully simple literalism assumed here would produce absurdities if applied consistently to other statements of Jesus. Those familiar with the language and imagery of the New Testament recognize at once the metaphorical nature of many expressions. The phrase "This is" frequently means no more than "this represents," or "this is like," or "this is a fulfillment of." For instance, Jesus, speaking of bread, said, "This is My body" (Matthew 26:26); and in reference to himself, "This is the bread . . . " (John 6:50).

Other examples of metaphor include "our God is a consuming fire" (Hebrews 12: 29) and "the rock was Christ" (I Corinthians 10:4). Surely the word is in such cases cannot be interpreted rigidly when it is used so fluidly by Jesus. (The classic example occurs in Matthew 12:50, where Jesus refers to a group of disciples as His "mother.") Careful students of the Bible have long observed this imagery in biblical writings, and have discovered that this fluid use of language is simply a literary device for communicating truths effectively. (This literary phenomenon is not limited to the Bible. For instance, in Shakespeare's play *The Merchant of Venice*, Shylock says of Portia, "A Daniel come to judgment: Yea, a Daniel!" (Act IV, Scene I).

Reincarnationists also misunderstand a similar statement concerning John the Baptist, "And he will go before him in the spirit and power of Elijah"(Luke 1:17, RSV*). This supposedly confirms the

Revised Standard Version.

claims of Matthew 11:14 and 17:10-13 that the Baptist was the reincarnation of the prophet. Such assertions are brought under grave suspicion when one observes the use of language in the biblical account of Elijah. 2 Kings 2:9-15, for example, reveals that going "in the spirit and power of Elijah" simply means being empowered by the same energy that empowered Elijah, that is, the Spirit of God. This is proved by the fact that the same phrasing is applied to a close worker of Elijah who succeeded him in his prophetic office, and of whom it is said, "The spirit of Elijah rests on Elisha"(v. 15).

Therefore, the most that can be inferred is that the role of Elijah was filled in a *functional* way by John the Baptist. So Jesus' statement about John the Baptist, rendered literally, would sound something like: "That which you were anticipating to be accomplished in the person of Elijah was virtually fulfilled in the person of John the Baptist, if you were perceptive enough to see it."

Finally, we must ask the reincarnationist: Why do you take notoriously obscure or difficult references as definitive and exclude all other passages that clearly deal with the subject of life after death? For there is in fact a significant number of texts where Jesus unambiguously teaches resurrection, not reincarnation.

"Born Again"

Another alleged example of reincarnationism in the Bible occurs in chapter three of the gospel of John, where Jesus tells the inquiring Nicodemus that he must be "born again." Since being "born again" is what reincarnation is all about, it is thought by some that Jesus was here alluding to that belief.

But this is a simple question of translation. The original Greek here is better translated "born from above." It is not being *born once more* that is of concern to Jesus, but rather being born into a *new quality of life*. Receiving "eternal life" in the teaching of Jesus means to be born into the family of God through following Jesus, and this fellowship is unbroken even by the intrusion of death. Immortality as such is not much of a concern in the gospels; it is living within the rule and reign of God, in a transformed and unending state of new life, that is important.

"Who Sinned?"

One of the more intriguing New Testament passages used by reincarnationists occurs in John 9. When they saw a man who was blind from birth, the disciples asked Jesus, "Rabbi, who sinned, this man or his parents, that he should be born blind?" Jesus responded by saying, "It was neither that this man sinned, nor his parents; but it was in order that the works of God might be displayed in Him" (vv. 2-3). This passage, it is said, confirms that Jesus and his disciples believed that it was possible for one to sin in some previous existence and to pay for that sin in another earthly life.

The second part of the disciples' question is explained by seeing that some Jewish rabbis had taken Exodus 20:5 to mean that the sins of the parents could leave their scar on the infant—a notion that Jesus rightly rejects here.

The first part is more difficult, because it appears to allow the possibility of the blind man having sinned before his birth. But again the rabbinical writings come to our aid: it was common in Judaism to find both those who believed in the (discarnate) preexistence of souls and those who taught that it was possible for one to be born handicapped because of sin committed prior to birth—not in some previous incarnation, but rather *while still in the womb!*[1]

Jesus in no way confirms the teaching of either reincarnationists or those rabbis; He simply affirms that the blind man had been prepared for a healing whose purpose was to glorify God. This meaning is not difficult to discern when the passage is studied in its original complex of ideas. If one is looking for some form of reincarnation in the Bible, it cannot be found in this passage.

"Whatever a Man Sows"

"For whatever a man sows, this he will also reap" (Galatians 6:7). Far from teaching the doctrines of karma and reincarnation, as some reincarnationists suppose, this text is actually one of the Bible's strongest statements of the doctrine of resurrection. If one looks at

1. H.L. Strack and P. Billerbeck, *Kommentar zum Neuen Testament aus Talmud und Midrasch*, vol. 2 (Munich: Beck, 1974), p. 527.

the entire passage from this letter of the apostle Paul, the true meaning emerges.

Do not be deceived, God is not mocked; for whatever a man sows, this he will also reap. For the one who sows to his own flesh shall from the flesh reap corruption, but the one who sows to the Spirit shall from the Spirit reap eternal life. (6:7-8)

Three Greek words in this passage help determine the text's meaning: *sarx, phthora,* and *pneuma.* *Sarx* is ordinarily translated "flesh," which is perhaps unfortunate, because *flesh* can also signify the physical body. This has given rise to the mistaken notion that the physical body is evil. *Flesh* often refers to that aspect of human life that is in rebellion against God and his purposes; for Paul the *flesh* and the *sinful heart* frequently are synonymous (see 5:19-21).

Phthora ("corruption"), in almost every instance of its occurrence in the New Testament, signifies that which is the result of the Fall—the decay and disintegration that is a consequence of human rebellion. All human, animal, and plant life is in bondage to *phthora* (cf. Romans 8:21; 1 Corinthians 15:42,50; Galatians 6:8; Colossians 2:22; 2 Peter 1:4; 2:12, 19). *Corruption* describes the present age, in contrast to the future transformation that God will bring about through re-creation and resurrection. Perhaps the most significant use of the word for our purposes can be seen in a passage that speaks very clearly of resurrection, 1 Corinthians 15 (see verses 42-50). Therefore, the one who sows the seeds of open rebellion against God by disregarding His eternal purposes will one day reap the fruit of that rebellion—disintegration and death on all levels of human existence.

In contrast to that terrible end, Paul speaks of the possibility of sowing to "the Spirit" (*pneuma*)—that is, the Spirit of God (see Galatians 6:8). To allow His Spirit to lead and transform one is to realize the "fruit of the Spirit" (5:22-23), something that occurs while one is still in the physical body.

Several important conclusions can now be drawn. (1) There is in the Galatians passage no dualism between the physical body and the immaterial part of man; rather the distinction is between life lived independently of God and life that is in harmony with His purposes and led by the Holy Spirit. (2) There are two destinies open to the human race: to follow the course of selfish rebellion and sink into ever lower levels of disintegration and decay, or to turn from this course and allow the Spirit of God to create a higher quality of life that is beyond the power of decay and death. This destiny will be fully realized and consummated in the resurrection body. (3) Far from teaching the doctrines of an impersonal karma and a mechanical reincarnation process, this passage speaks clearly of the justice and holiness of a personal God who destines His creation to perfection and completion.

"Before I Formed You in the Womb I Knew You"

Frequently, apologists for reincarnation point to biblical passages that speak of God's knowing individuals before their birth. One example is found in Jeremiah: "Now the word of the Lord came to me saying, 'Before I formed you in the womb I knew you, and before you were born I consecrated you'" (1:4-5). This idea is not uncommon in the Bible, and even the apostle Paul affirms it for himself (Galatians 1:15).

But these texts cannot be used to argue the preexistence of Jeremiah or Paul; they, like all the prophetic books, speak of no more than God's foreknowledge: "I am God, and there is no one like Me, declaring the end from the beginning and from ancient times things which have not been done" (Isaiah 46:9-10). God, according to the writers of the Bible, knew all things and all people even before they existed; He knew who and what He was going to create from the beginning. Even a moderate amount of reading in the rabbis and in the Old Testament will make this quite clear.

Further, the language of foreknowledge in the Bible is often tied to the doctrine that God chose an entire nation, Israel, to be a people for Himself (Deuteronomy 7:6-8; Psalm 135:4; Isaiah 41:8f; et al). Thus, those who argue that there is biblical evidence for individual preexistence logically must also admit to the preexistence of an entire nation.

Melchizedek

It is claimed by some that Jesus was the reincarnation of the mysterious Melchizedek, a person mentioned only twice in the Old Testament (Genesis 14 and Psalm 110) and once in the New Testament (Hebrews 7), where his priesthood is said to be similar to that of Jesus.

This argument is too farfetched to deserve much space, since Melchizedek clearly is seen only as a prototype of Jesus' *priestly* function, and the comparison stops there. The Bible, silent as regards Melchizedek's ancestry or fate, speaks volumes on that of Jesus. Undoubtedly, all that is intended in this comparison is to say that Jesus' office as priest or intermediary endures forever and cannot be passed on to anyone else.

"Biblical evidence" for reincarnation amounts to little more than a short catalogue of difficult Bible references, references that are sufficiently difficult to court misunderstanding or incomprehension. This will become even clearer in the following pages, where both the teaching of resurrection and the overall view of the New Testament will be examined.

Resurrection

6

The Doctrine of Salvation

In the end, arguing with reincarnationists over this or that isolated text misses the main point, for the total conceptual world of the New Testament is far removed from that of reincarnationists.

Throughout the New Testament there is a fundamental agreement about the doctrine of salvation, which is everywhere seen as an act of unmerited favor based on God's saving work through Jesus Christ. The apostle Paul expresses it in confessional form: "Christ died for our sins according to the Scriptures" (1 Corinthians 15:3).

Virtually everything written on the subject of reincarnation speaks of salvation by works: one can pay off one's "karmic debt," thereby securing a better position in the next life, by working hard in this life. Salvation (if one may call it that) is a reward for one's own efforts. It might be said that the notion of salvation by works is even more fundamental to popular reincarnation theory than the doctrine of successive lives: these lives are just the necessary fields in which the labor can be accomplished.

All this runs directly counter to the view of salvation that Jesus and His apostles taught. All our best efforts and finest performances, they said, are utterly worthless and ineffective in securing salvation; in fact, they actually work against us because they are no more than expressions of our pride and self-sufficiency. Moreover, due to our fallen condition—our rebellious stance against a personal God and His will—we are completely powerless to do anything about our lostness. We are imprisoned and must be set free by some force outside ourselves, by some act of God on our behalf.

Therefore, the number of our earthly lives is irrelevant to salvation, since God is completely unimpressed by our attempts to pay off a debt that He alone could and did pay on the cross of Jesus Christ.

Furthermore, the theory of reincarnation has an implicit contempt for incarnation itself, since it views the body as essentially evil. The believer's ultimate goal is a state of nonincarnation, or life without a body.

This view is radically different from that of the Bible, which sees the body as fundamentally good, though corrupted by the Fall. Nowhere does it teach that the physical body is evil; rather, Scriptures affirm that it is the creation of God and is, therefore, good. Evil comes not from the physical body but from the corrupted heart and mind of a fallen race.

The great thinker G.K. Chesterton pointed out generations ago that Eastern philosophy inevitably leads to contempt for life, whereas a Judaeo-Christian view leads to contempt for death.[1] In biblical terms it is death that is the enemy, not life; it is existence in a noncorruptible *body* that is our final, hoped-for state—not existence without a body.

The biblical conception of redemption is not *escape from* the material, but *invasion of* the earthly and physical by the spiritual and eternal. God's goal for His creation is not to obliterate it but to transform it and restore it, for originally it was created good; and it has fallen not because it was physical but because it was in rebellion.

This invasion, and therefore the restoration of God's good creation, is heralded by the resurrection of Jesus Christ. To deepen our understanding of the nature of salvation, we shall now look more closely at His resurrection.

1. G.K. Chesterton, *Orthodoxy* (Garden City, N.Y.: Image, 1959).

7

Resurrection in the New Testament

The Example of Christ

The resurrection of Jesus Christ was not a simple revivification, the mere return to life of a corpse. When Christ rose from the
dead, His body was raised to a higher level of existence—a level in
continuity with, but not limited to, His former bodily form.

The New Testament accounts are clear and consistent when
they tell about Christ's resurrection body. When He was raised from
the dead, the gospels affirm that the tomb was empty; the crucified
body was gone. Jesus, then, did not come back in a body that was
utterly unrelated to His earthly body. The body that suffered and was
hanged on the cross was *transformed* and raised from death's grip; and
so the New Testament affirms that the redemption that Jesus brings is
not mere retreat from physical life into pure spiritual life. His
redemption is a comprehensive work, including both the physical
and the spiritual dimensions of human life.

It is interesting that after the Easter event much of the
narrative is taken up, especially in Luke, with trying to persuade
people that Jesus' resurrection body was recognizably *His*, even
bearing the visible marks of the cross. Christian tradition specifically
counters any notion that the resurrection body was any less physical

61

than the preresurrection body. In fact, it was *more* substantial. As the flower is more than its seed, and the butterfly more than its larva, so the resurrected person is more substantial and glorious than he was in his former state.

Jesus' resurrection can be contrasted with the experience of Lazarus, recorded in John 11. Lazarus was brought back to life by Jesus after being in the tomb for four days. He returned essentially the same man, with all his prior strengths and weaknesses. The rest of his life was an interlude, granted by Jesus in order to say something about His power over death.

It is probably not at all correct to refer to the raising of Lazarus as a "resurrection." Revivification is not resurrection. The ultimate model for the resurrected life is that of Jesus Christ, and we should not attempt to look outside the Easter event for our definition.

The Message of Christ

While we know little about the resurrection of the lost, Jesus taught clearly that *all* will be resurrected—both those destined to eternal blessing and those destined to condemnation (John 5:28-29). The ultimate state of a person depends entirely upon his relationship to Jesus Christ (John 3:16; 11:25).

One of the most intriguing parables of Jesus is the story of Lazarus and the rich man, found in Luke 16:19-31. Despite some diversity of opinion concerning this parable, it seems clear that Jesus here holds out no hope for more than a single life on this imperfect earth; indeed, He indicates that it would do no good even to allow men more time in the one life that they do have.

An important element of Jesus' thought concerning life after death emerges in His discussion with Sadducees, who denied resurrection (Luke 20:35-36). Here Jesus argues that one remains alive even though one's physical body is dead. And after resurrection, at least with respect to those who are destined to eternal blessing and glory, it is impossible for one to die more than once. In the mind of Jesus, one's state after death is not open to revision; this single physical life is the only arena in which the eternal future can be determined.

It is important to notice that this same view of *one death for all time* is picked up and developed in exactly that document that we are finding to be one of the earliest expositions of the teaching of Jesus, the letter to the Hebrews.

> Just as man is destined to die once, and after that to face judgement, so Christ was sacrificed once to take away the sins of many people; and He will appear a second time, not to bear sin, but to bring salvation to those who are waiting for Him. (Hebrews 9:27-28, NIV*)

This passage clearly teaches that a person dies *once*. Some reincarnationists argue that this means *once per lifetime*, so that one may live many lives, each of which is ended by one death. It is important that we do not allow personal preference to determine our point of view here; we must look at the grammar and syntax of the text for the answer. The Greek word for "once," as well as the context of this passage, demands that the meaning be *once for all time*, and not once now and again later (cf.1 Peter 3:18).

Further, the apostle Paul, acknowledged by the early church as the preserver and interpreter of Jesus' teaching, admits in Philippians 1:23 that he is hard pressed between two possibilities, either dying and being with Christ or remaining in this life. For Paul, a rabbi accepting the assumptions of many other rabbis in these matters, "to depart" meant to go from this earthly, physical tabernacle to one's respective place, either in or out of the favor of God. The favor of God meant for Paul to be with Christ for eternity, unavailable for perpetual recycling. He believed in resurrection in a recreated body that in a sense was in substantial continuity with the old body, but that was free from sin and death and other restrictions of the present order. This perfect and indestructible eternal body would constitute the final state of existence.

More light is shed on the nature of the resurrection body in Paul's second letter to the church in Corinth. He speaks of being "naked" immediately after death(2 Corinthians 5:3)—a temporary condition, not an ultimate destination or goal—and looks forward to "a building from God, a house not made with hands, eternal in the heavens" (v. 1). This is the resurrection body, the state of existence that is suited for the age to come and its transformed, transfigured earth. Paul believes in a mortal body and an immortal body, but nowhere mentions an immortal soul.

New International Version.

Paul, in accord with other biblical writers, looks forward to a redeemed, transformed earth with people living in transformed bodies adapted to their new quality of existence. Whereas this quality of life begins now for the believer, the consummation of the new life awaits the new, resurrected body. This spiritual body is not a discorporate spirit but a true body, fitted for the new age on a transformed earth.

The Nature of the Resurrection Body

We tend by habit of mind to regard our present physical bodies as the extreme end of the range of possibilities, with pure spirit as the other extreme; and we think that somehow the resurrection state will be somewhere between the two. We find it hard to believe that some future state could be at least as real, substantial, or "body-like" as what we now experience. But in fact the resurrection body represents the extreme end. Our present state is actually the mid-range condition. In comparison to the resurrection state our bodies presently are, as it were, as a mist or a vapor.

This New Testament insistence upon a bodily future existence reaffirms that we are not mere spiritual fragments of an impersonal god, trapped in "evil" physical bodies, trying to work our way back to our source. We do not simply *have* bodies, we *are* bodies, and we live in personal relation to God, who created us as beings separate from Himself.

Resurrection and Creation

In the Bible, the end of history is seen in the light of the beginning of history. Resurrection, then, has much to say about God's creation.

The Old Testament affirms that all life and matter is the result of divine creation out of nothing. God made that which is, and without Him there could be nothing. No raw material or preexistent building blocks were necessary in order to create—God's power brought something out of nothing.

The theme of creation is also seen in the Bible's view of history's end. The New Testament suggests that just as God created the universe and all that is in it, so He will continue His work after its end. The "new heaven and new earth" (Revelation 21:1) will be the result of God's creative power: He shall re-create or restore to life and existence that which has died, decayed, or disintegrated.

To affirm the resurrection of the body is to affirm the value of God's creation. The doctrines of creation and resurrection do not exist independently of each other; they are incoherent apart from each other. Together, they show the meaning and purpose of God's creating bodily life and then bringing about its full redemption and consummation.

Resurrection, then, is not a natural stage in life's development; it is an act of intrusion, of God's breaking in with a new burst of creation. Whereas on one level it affirms a continuity between the two states, nevertheless it represents—perhaps paradoxically—a quantum leap upward, an advance far out of proportion to anything the original bodily form would lead us to expect. Resurrection always must be on the order of a surprise.

In World War II it was not uncommon for important persons to be captured and confined in an enemy prison camp. The Allies were then faced with the difficult problem of rescuing those people without risking the lives of many people. Occasionally they would send one person, highly trained in the art of escape, to infiltrate the camp and devise a sophisticated plan to break out, with the other prisoners following safely behind.

We are much like those prisoners in need of rescue. We are trapped in a position of separation and alienation from our homeland and our God. Our own rebellion has made us unable to free ourselves. Left to our own devices, we all surely will die in the most degraded conditions imaginable. But someone has been sent into our situation to save us, someone so specially qualified that only He can liberate us. In one bold move He has broken through the boundaries of life, death, and sin and has called out to us, and all those with us, declaring that to follow Him is life, health, and repatriation. To stay and rely on ourselves is certain death. He has tunneled through for us, and we are to follow Him out into the bright sunlight of God's care and forgiveness. The risen Christ is indeed the "pioneer" of our salvation (Hebrews 2:10, RSV).

8

The Case for Resurrection

The case for resurrection presented in this chapter is not, like the case for reincarnation, based on an accumulation of empirical data. Nor does it begin as the case for resurrection in general, as opposed to reincarnation in general. Rather, it gives evidences for *one* case of resurrection in history, at one particular point in time: the resurrection of Jesus Christ.

This difference in method illustrates a principal difference between the apologetics of reincarnation and that of resurrection. The case for reincarnation lies purely in the accumulation of human data suggestive of the theory. The strength and credibility of the case for resurrection is located in the credibility and authenticity of a single major event in history, and the case stands or falls on whether or not that event actually took place.

Even though many Jewish people believed in a resurrection of sorts before Jesus' ministry began—a hope based on a handful of faint allusions in the Old Testament and bits and pieces from the intertestamental writings—it was the resurrection of Jesus Christ that was seen to be of such finality and decisiveness to the believing community that it immediately came to be the premise of the specifically Christian proclamation and defense.

The argument of this chapter runs as follows: (1) Jesus Christ taught resurrection as the destiny of the entire human race and claimed unique authority to speak of these matters. (2) Jesus' teaching and authority were vindicated by His own resurrection. The historical evidence for the life, ministry, death, and resurrection of Jesus is substantial enough not only to warrant serious attention but to compel confidence in it. (3) The documents that preserve for us the story of the resurrection are demonstrably reliable, and the strength of the manuscript evidence of the New Testament matches or exceeds that of any literature ever to come out of the Graeco-Roman world.

Jesus' Teachings and Claims of Unique Authority

According to the New Testament, Jesus taught resurrection as the destiny of all, and viewed Himself as qualified to teach authoritatively on matters of life and death, because of His unique character and personhood.

Among other things, Christ is depicted as "the one in whom is manifested" the Creator of the universe; the fullest disclosure of the character and person of God; the focal point of all that God had been doing in history; the chief personality in God's creation of the world; the ruler of natural forces; the watershed of human destiny; and the only path to the presence of God. Jesus is portrayed not simply as the greatest teacher, but as the foundation of all teaching—that is, truth itself.

These assertions are so staggering in their nature and comprehensiveness that it has led some thinkers to say that there are only three logical possibilities: (a) He could have been a lunatic far beyond the scope of any other; (b) He could have been a liar attempting to deceive the populace, knowing full well the absurdity of His claims; or (c) He could have been sane and honest—in fact, what He claimed to be, the Lord of all history.[1] If He was not the Lord, then He surely could not have qualified as a "good man" or a prophet, since prophets and good men do not tell extravagant lies about themselves.

There is a striking difference between the New Testament

1. C.S. Lewis, *Mere Christianity* (Glasgow: William Collins Sons & Co., 1982), p. 52.

and other ancient documents that describe great people. The main thrust of Christ's ministry was not to offer some new teaching to humanity, nor to set up some kingdom on earth to *out-do* all other kingdoms, nor to set in motion a revolution in society; rather, Jesus said that He came primarily *to die*. He came to die, and His death would have lasting impact upon the lives and deaths of all creatures of the earth for all time. This has appeared to many people an extraordinary thing, since no great leader makes death his greatest work. Death was not to the first-century Jews the way to go about demonstrating victory, especially the victory of God the Creator. However, Jesus insisted that in His death and in the events to follow that death the world would be transformed, and all of life charged with new meaning.

The Historical Evidence

Many early witnesses testify that the same Jesus who lived, performed miracles, and claimed authority for Himself actually died according to His own predictions, that on the third day His tomb was empty as He had also predicted, and that He appeared to a great number of people over a period of forty days. In fact, those who had seen the risen Jesus Christ exceeded five hundred people (1 Corinthians 15:6).

It is evident to a reader of the New Testament that the Easter event was the cornerstone of early Christian preaching and apologetic. It was generally understood that the resurrection vindicated all that Jesus said and did; it was the final imprimatur of God the Creator. The earliest preaching affirmed that if Jesus had not been raised from the dead, then all that the disciples had believed about Him was actually in vain. All the integrity of the gospel hinged on the truth of this event, and decidedly not on a handful of philosophical and moral teachings.

The Manuscript Evidence

It is often thought that the New Testament documents are of a rather late vintage, written long after the events they report and composed by simple, mythically-disposed minds. However, this view is not sustained by any serious study of the documents themselves, and many of those who have set out on this journey of investigation have ended their quest by becoming strong advocates of the manuscripts they had sought to discredit.

General Lew Wallace, one of the great statesmen of his time, traveled to Palestine seeking completely to dispel the myth of the New Testament story once for all. But in so doing he was over-whelmed by the strength of evidence for the resurrection of Jesus Christ and returned home to pen the great biblical epic *Ben Hur*.

Sir William Ramsay, one of the greatest archaeologists of Asia Minor in modern history, at first doubted the veracity of the New Testament manuscripts. But after being overpowered by the weight of evidence, he became one of the chief proponents of the New Testament records for the rest of his life.

Those familiar with the study of archaeology or textual criticism will recognize at once the names of Sir Frederic Kenyon and W.F. Albright, who towered over their respective fields and were firm believers in the essential reliability of the New Testament.

Testimonies from authorities such as those may be piled one upon the other, and the reader need only consult the list of sources in the back of this book for additional study.[2] What follows is but a brief sketch of the manuscript evidence.

First, it is safe to say that the New Testament documents have proved themselves as substantially trustworthy records of the first century in those areas where they have been tested by other sources. They are historically accurate accounts of the events they report, although they do exhibit some of the usual historical and manuscript difficulties. The days of having to "prove the Bible" are gone.

Second, the documents surpass any others from the Graeco-Roman world in the number of surviving manuscripts. Whereas in the investigation of classical Greek literature a scholar may be working with only a handful of manuscripts (a few hundred, or in some cases even one or two), in the case of the New Testament one must work through well over 5,000 Greek manuscripts and fragments of manuscripts.

2. See for examples: F.F. Bruce, *The New Testament Documents: Are They Reliable?* (Grand Rapids: Eerdmans, 1968); John Warwick Montgomery, *History and Christianity* (Downers Grove, Ill.: InterVarsity, 1965); John A.T. Robinson, *Can We Trust the New Testament?* (Grand Rapids: Eerdmans, 1977).

And third, the New Testament's textual gap—the amount of time between the actual event and the date of the first document that we possess—is far shorter than that of other ancient writings. Whereas many centuries usually separate events from the earliest secular Greek manuscripts describing those events, in the case of the New Testament the gap is only a few centuries. In comparison with other textual traditions, the gap in years for the New Testament documents is so small as to be negligible.

Whereas only a few generations ago it was commonly believed that the documents were rather late productions of the church, usually written in the name of an apostle sometime after his death, recent studies both within and without the Christian community suggest that the New Testament was virtually completed before the death of the original eyewitnesses. In other words, by the time of the destruction of Jerusalem in A.D. 70, the documents, with perhaps a few exceptions, were complete and in circulation.[3]

The importance of this cannot be overstated. If the New Testament had been written well after the death of the original eyewitnesses, who would have been around to correct any false reports, exaggerations, or patent untruths? But it appears that the documents enjoyed the distinct advantage of having the correcting influence not only of the community of faith, but also of the hostile community, who would have been delighted to catch the Christian believers making assertions about Jesus that were untrue.

Finally, there is another line of defense for the biblical texts that is not available for other ancient literature, namely, the writings of the church Fathers. These men lived during the few centuries that constitute the textual gap. They alluded to or quoted from the New Testament so often that, even if no New Testament texts had survived, we would still have virtually the entire New Testament preserved for us.

Therefore, it is no exaggeration to assert that the New Testament text is far better attested to than any of the ancient writings by such prominent figures as Caesar, Livy, Herodotus, Thucydides, and Tacitus.[4] (One could add to this list the Hindu

3. Robinson, p. 63.

Vedas and *Bhagavadgita,* as well as the *Koran.*) These facts are not a mystery to anyone who is involved in the field of textual criticism, and they are easily accessible to any inquirer through a well-stocked university library.

Any successful rebuttal of these arguments must discover a flaw in one of the three main pieces of evidence. It must show either that Jesus did not teach, as if He were one who had authority, one life, judgment and resurrection; or that there is not good historical evidence for Christ's resurrection; or that the New Testament manuscripts are not reliable. Thus far no one has done any of these successfully.

It can therefore be demonstrated that we possess a responsible eyewitness testimony about a man who overshadowed all other human beings in power and authority, and who clearly stated that He alone is the definitive teacher in the areas of human life, human death, and human destiny; and that this testimony is preserved in some of the best attested manuscripts ever to come out of the ancient world.

4. Bruce, pp. 16ff.

9
Summary

The theory of reincarnation is attractive to many people in the Western world who know little about its Eastern roots and its social and political consequences in the Eastern countries where it prevails. In an age of unreflective, aimless materialism, it appears to affirm the value and importance of people. It is a coherent and convenient belief system that avoids the uncomfortable matters of guilt and responsibility before a personal and righteous God. In its adaptation to the American scene, it has come to reflect many of the moods and fashionable beliefs of our generation.

There are many possible definitions of reincarnation. No attempt has been made to deal carefully with the most ancient formulations, but rather to focus on that hybrid form of the theory that has sprouted in American soil in this century.

Reincarnation's chief points of departure from the classical Christian view of life after death are (1) its contention that there is more than one earthly, physical life in which to shape or influence one's destiny, and (2) its radically different conception of salvation.

The concept of karma, which puts the individual in the position of carving out his own future lives through effort in this life, is in reality simply another expression of self-sufficiency and pride. It casts the individual as his own savior; and on this basis it is implicitly

73

condemned in the biblical tradition.

Closely related to the popular conception of karma is the notion that all of us are innately capable of doing the good and the right, and that it is simply ignorance—and not sin—that keeps us from realizing this innate goodness. This view has difficulty producing a mutually agreed upon standard of right and wrong, since it lacks the presence of a personal God.

Imported into American reincarnationism are the twin ideas of evolutionary spiritual advance and blind optimism about the human race. Such a rosy optimism about the ultimate end of all things must come face-to-face with the stubborn facts of the universe.

Except for a small minority who hold out some possibility of believing in the personal God of the Bible while at the same time believing in reincarnation theory, most admit that the mind and heart of reincarnation philosophy is monism, the faith that every part of the universe is one with Ultimate Reality. Thus, the destiny of everything is a reunion with this impersonal oneness, a state which is virtually indistinguishable from what others call "nothingness."

Monism nurtures a pride of immortality by assigning to the soul properties that are inherent to it rather than received from a personal Creator who consciously sustains existence. For the reincarnationist, the soul is the focal point of salvation. The soul is thought of as sharply separate from the body, which is considered a second-class aspect of the human being. The Bible, on the other hand, sees both soul and body (or rather, nonmaterial and material aspects) as created by God and therefore potential recipients of His redemption.

Proof for the theory of reincarnation is made up principally of experiences of retrocognition (knowledge of the past with no naturally explainable basis). While the theory of reincarnation is congruous with evidence of retrocognition, the evidence is not necessarily congruous with the theory; in other words, reincarnation theory cannot live without retrocognition, but retrocognition can live without reincarnation theory. Psychic research abounds with examples of retrocognition that make the theory of reincarnation unnecessary. Thus, there is no reason to believe that so-called memories of past lives are memories at all.

All the thousand examples of "past life recall" that can be gathered together cannot outweigh this logical argument. If the best and most dramatic instances of retrocognition can be easily understood within a nonreincarnational framework, then the lesser cases—no matter how many are adduced—cannot successfully support the theory.

With fascinating consistency, the demonic as an alternative explanation for past-life recall and for the strange cases involving birth-marks has been studiously avoided. Why, when discussing the possibility that spirit possession may account for some "memories," is demonic possession not even considered? There are evil *incarnate* personalities who shock us with their deception and ferocity, so why is it unthinkable that there might be evil *discarnate* personalities who impose themselves upon our world and experience? The questions have not been properly addressed by the reincarnationist community.

The expanding field of death-and-dying research has not shed much light upon the question of reincarnation or resurrection. In its present state, the evidence is too scanty and too open to distortion based on the researcher's assumptions. Only special pleading and question-begging can construe the evidence to make it appear friendly toward the theory of reincarnation.

Biblical evidence for reincarnation is merely the product of wishful thinking and faulty literary criticism. Reincarnation has never been a part either of the Old or the New Testaments; it was never part of the teaching of Jesus or His disciples, as both textual analysis and background examination clearly reveal. Reincarnation is alien to every kind of biblical thought and expression.

The teaching of resurrection found in the New Testament is closely linked to the doctrine of salvation as taught by Jesus and the early apostles. Both the textual form and the content of the documents speak uncompromisingly of one life lived in the present order, one death of the physical body for all time and for all people, and one resurrection of the individual to face judgment by a holy, personal God. From the viewpoint of the Bible, soul and body—if indeed those are the proper divisions of the human creation—are both objects of God's redemption; and if they are parted at death, it is God's intention that they be reunited either for judgment or in a glorious, transformed state in His presence.

The case for resurrection is the case for the resurrection of Jesus Christ. The resurrection of the believer, which is seen in the New Testament as the only form of death's survival in the truest sense, is founded upon a tripod of logic: Jesus taught resurrection; He was raised from death, which among other things vindicated His teaching; and the sources that preserve the story of His life, death, and resurrection are historically reliable and trustworthy accounts.

10
Conclusion

If belief in reincarnation is held with any seriousness at all, it inevitably leads to the acceptance of virtually the whole of the monistic or Eastern view of life. Without karma, the belief in many lives is incomprehensible, and part and parcel of the doctrine of karma are the notions of upward spiritual progress attained through one's own efforts and the movement toward ultimate oneness with the universe.

All serious believers in reincarnation do not necessarily see themselves as Hindus in the formal sense, but their thinking is influenced by what monism implies, and their beliefs determine their behavior.

This belief is destructive to the personal life from a biblical perspective, since it obliterates the felt need for repentance, forgiveness, and transformation by the Holy Spirit. It is equally destructive on the social and political level.

P.J. Thomas, writing about popular Hinduism in his own homeland of India, demonstrates how fatalism, lack of concern for the suffering of others, general inaction and even various forms of

---

1. P.J. Thomas, *Hindu Religion, Customs and Manners* (Bombay: D.B. Taraporevala, Sons & Co., Ltd., 1950), pp. 39-40, 70, 151.

blind cruelty can often be traced to the two doctrines of reincarnation and karma.[1] Mark Albrecht shows how murders, death in all its guises, the reduction and sacking of cities, wars, and the complete denial of both absolute and relative moral values in society have all been justified on the basis of these same teachings.[2]

In view of what history tells us about the influence of these doctrines, one may venture to guess what would happen if they became guiding principles for people in critical positions—by the congressman facing a piece of legislation on the poor and under-priveleged, by the judge trying to decide how to sentence a violent criminal, or by the hospital chaplain who is asked by a dying patient to explain death. Such questions could be raised in virtually every area of life.

Beliefs are powerful. They are never "mere" beliefs. They drive armies, create and pull down empires, spark or retard the advancement of nations. This is particularly true when the beliefs are religious.

Therefore if Eastern notions about life and death are accepted, then the end product will be a complete and total revolution in areas such as political thought, social policy, and legal reform. It would not be changing course; it would be changing ships. Eventually, it would not be simply changing views on the world; it would be changing worlds. For what reincarnationism and Hinduism have produced in Asia will in many ways be produced again wherever they are planted; seeds will always give birth to the same tree, wherever they are allowed to grow. It is necessary therefore to consider seriously which side of this issue we will be on, for the view that predominates will determine history for us all.

In the final analysis, there are only three serious options for belief as regards what happens after death: materialism, which holds that there is absolutely nothing after death; reincarnationism, which is essentially the Eastern understanding of existence; and the

2. Mark Albrecht, *Reincarnation: A Christian Appraisal* (Downer's Grove, Ill.: InterVarsity, 1982), pp. 103-4.

Christian view that resurrection and judgment await us all.

The materialist, who denies reality outside the world of matter, once enjoyed the reputation of being the honest thinker, unimpressed by anything except "hard fact." However, with a sizeable portion of the academic community paying closer attention to research on death and dying, he has become a relic of nineteenth-century science and philosophy. Strict materialism is simply no longer as fashionable as it once was.

The reincarnationist, as we have seen, clings to a theory whose credentials are highly dubious at best—and at worst, exceedingly dangerous both on the private and public levels.

It is surprising, perhaps, that so few alternative answers to the question of existence after death are on the idea market. For many people, none of them is desirable. This limitation of choices is further aggravated because two of them, namely materialism and Hinduism, are philosophically members of the same family.

For they are in reality merely two sides of the same monistic coin; ultimately, both are simple reductions of all that is to only one reality. Both deny half of creation; both virtually affirm the oblivion of the human personality as we know it; and practically, both have led to a devaluation of human life. One looks to monism—be it modern science or ancient religious piety—in vain for any help for our troubled world.

Resurrection seems to be the least comfortable of the three options. Some Christian believers have confessed that they came to believe in resurrection not because it was the most appealing to their tastes, or the most naturally attractive to them, or because they thought "this is the way it ought to be," but only because the case for resurrection was the most rational and compelling.

The doctrine of resurrection remains with us so stubbornly because it comes to us with so much authority. Its credentials surpass that of any other framework for understanding death and life. It forces itself upon us, frequently against our sensibilities, natural inclinations, and perhaps even our wishes; but not against our reason, conscience, or historical judgment. It stands not on the character or reputation of a handful of intellectuals or scholars, but upon the truth of Jesus Christ. The doctrine of resurrection stands not because the church teaches it; the church teaches it because the doctrine stands. It speaks to us so forcefully because in it God Himself speaks and declares to us that He raised Jesus from the dead and that He will raise us up in the Last Day.

Questions and Answers

The following pages contain answers to the questions most commonly asked in public exchanges on the subject of reincarnation. Some of these questions are not exclusively confined to the reincarnation debate, but represent issues often on the minds of those who are interested in the topic.

How can one lifetime of only sixty or seventy years be determinative of all eternity?

This question seems to have some merit, for it appears grossly out of proportion that a handful of years on this earth could determine the eternal destiny of any person. But the merit is only on the surface, since the assumptions behind the question are far more difficult to defend than the biblical position.

The first assumption hidden away in this question is that somehow it makes good sense to compare thousands of years or more with eternity, but not seventy years. But this is very much like saying, "The ant seems so small compared to the size of the earth, let's try a larger ant." Whether one compares seventy years or seventy thousand years with infinity, the time will always be infinitesimally small compared to unending existence.

Moreover, it is common to see small, seemingly insignificant choices resulting in the most catastrophic ends. The airline pilot who has a drink before takeoff and ends up killing hundreds of people; the angry driver whose impatience on the freeway causes a fully-loaded school bus to plunge down a ravine; or even the assassination of an archduke that triggers a world war: all are examples of the disproportion between misdeed and outcome with which we are all painfully aware. This sort of thing occurs with monotonous frequency in the daily news. Life is full of such examples, and it would not be an exaggeration to say that history may be regarded as a chronicle of such disproportions.

Another wrong assumption behind this question is that people will naturally make wiser choices and more responsible decisions as they grow in years and experience, particularly if the years are multiplied by an abundance of earthly lives.

Surely this optimism regarding the human spirit is hard to maintain in the face of what we know about history, or even about ourselves. We find the wise and the foolish among children, adults, and the very old alike; wisdom and responsibility have little to do with chronological age or amount of experience. And one frequently finds a greater response to the gospel among the young, whereas the multiplication of years commonly results in a more firmly entrenched resistance to Christ, as well as increased hostility toward the idea of repentance. It is very difficult to imagine why centuries of life would predispose one more toward the gospel of Jesus than would one lifetime, but it would be quite easy to imagine the spiritual eye growing frightfully more dim, and the spiritual ear growing less attuned to the truth. This view is not incongruous with the history of a human race that has by no means become less greedy, ferocious, and deceptive with the passing of the centuries.

HAS NOT THE CHURCH SUPPRESSED REINCARNATIONAL THOUGHT?

Reincarnationists are fond of asserting that reincarnation was once a part of biblical teaching, but that the doctrine was surreptitiously removed by crafty editors or church councils.[1]

Such beliefs are notable only for their lack of historical integrity. A brief survey of the available evidence will show that it would make no difference what later church councils decided, because one can go directly to the most ancient texts that preserve the gospel for us. Those texts that are the earliest surviving manuscripts in Greek show that the verities of the faith antedate any medieval attempts at revision. Many of these manuscripts are *older* than the major councils of the church. The ancient world was so flooded with copies of the New Testament that it was well beyond the power of any officials to expunge certain uncomfortable doctrines from them. Therefore, we know with a high degree of certainty what the New Testament said about many different issues before such councils were even held. This kind of documentary criticism is indefensible.

It is surprising to discover how many people believe this conspiracy theory of the Bible. It is an emotion-charged view that casts the church in the role of "Grand Inquisitor," covering up here, censuring there, hurling anathemas everywhere. This comic-book portrayal of the history of doctrine is usually supported by favorite examples of the church's resistance to new ideas, frequently in the

---

1. Joseph Head and S.L. Cranston, *Reincarnation: The Phoenix Fire Mystery* (New York: Warner Books, 1977), p. 134.

area of scientific discovery. Instances in which the church persecuted popular heresies are dragged up. But there is no proof that suppression occurred with respect to the question of reincarnation.

The observation that the church has often resisted ideas that are new or different from established dogma is a critique not so much of the church as it is of human nature in general. People of every generation have tended to be intransigent and stubborn in the face of different ideas or new discoveries, as a brief survey of the history of science will quickly reveal. Many of those who were condemned or censured by churchmen for their discoveries were themselves Christians (e.g. Galileo, Copernicus, and others) who were carrying out their investigations in the belief that, since God was the Creator, anything they could discover about creation was of Him and was therefore good. (In fact, that was the philosophical framework out of which modern science emerged, following hard on the heels of the Reformation.) So, to say that Christians have censured new and different ideas is only to say that Christians tend to be like everyone else when it comes to new ideas and discoveries.

Moreover, Christians have *opposed*—not "covered up" or "suppressed"—the theory of reincarnation, because it is directly antithetical to the teaching of Jesus regarding life, death, resurrection, and eternal existence. The accusation of suppression rings hollow. The two views of survival beyond death are simply incompatible with each other, and to hold one is quite naturally to oppose the other. To hold one view of something and to reject its opposite cannot properly be called "suppression" or "censure." No doubt certain churchmen throughout the ages have censured and suppressed, just as human beings have done since the beginning. But there is no connection between that fact and the origins of Christian thought. It is best to put aside notions of conspiracies, inquisitions, and censures, and simply to deal with the beliefs of resurrection and reincarnation from an evidential point of view.

DOES NOT THE EVIDENCE FROM HYPNOTIC REGRESSION SUPPORT REINCARNATION?

Hypnotic regression, or retrocognition under hypnosis, is in principle no different from retrocognition achieved under other circumstances, except that it is probably less reliable.[2] It has been established that such knowledge of the past is a reality, and that many people have experienced it. But the fact that it occurs under hypnosis rather than during a conscious state is no more a support for reincarnation than any other form of retrocognition.

Even among those like Ian Stevenson, who do careful research in the hope of supporting reincarnation, hypnotic regression is not held in high honor when compared to careful cross-examination of individuals who are fully conscious.

Hypnotic regression is under double suspicion because of the gold mine it is becoming for practitioners—particularly those who practice "past life therapy"—and because of the vulnerability of their patients.

IS NOT BELIEF IN REINCARNATION MUCH OLDER THAN BELIEF IN RESURRECTION?

It is a common assumption that since Hinduism arose a few thousand years before Christianity, the idea of reincarnation must be the earliest and therefore the most time-honored and credible view.

There are two difficulties with this view. First, even if it could be shown that the idea of reincarnation was the earlier of the two, that still would not be any reason for accepting it over the idea of resurrection. The relative age of an idea plays no particular role in establishing its believability.

Moreover, it probably is not true that reincarnation is the more ancient. Hinduism is much older than Christianity, but it is not at all clear when reincarnation became part of it; about 300 B.C. is perhaps the best guess.[3] Christianity, on the other hand, did not have to incorporate resurrection into its teaching. Rather, Christianity sprang out of resurrection—the resurrection of Jesus Christ. If there had not been a resurrection of Jesus, there would have been no Christianity to teach.

But this was not the advent of the idea of resurrection. The

2. Stevenson, *Twenty Cases Suggestive of Reincarnation* (New York American Society for Psychical Research, 1966), p. 3.
3. Mark Albrecht, *Reincarnation: A Christian Appraisal* (Downer's Grove, Ill.: InterVarsity, 1982), p. 27.

concept appears frequently in the intertestamental literature (the writings between the close of the Old Testament and the opening of the New Testament), and there are allusions and references to it in the Old Testament itself (e.g., Isaiah 26:19; Daniel 12:2; Hosea 6:2).

However, this question is not particularly helpful, since for our purposes the doctrines must stand or fall on their own merits. Any attempt to appraise them chronologically is beside the point.

Can a christian believe in reincarnation?

This seemingly straightforward question is actually relatively ambiguous, although the answer quite clearly is no. It is ambiguous simply because the word *Christian* has lost virtually all meaning in our culture. The word once had some specific content, serving to denote a follower of Jesus Christ, as depicted and clarified in the New Testament. But today the word has been bandied about in so many varied and unclear ways that even to use it at all necessitates spending an afternoon defining it.

If a "Christian" is simply a person who in some way identifies with Jesus, or is in sympathy with what he understands to be Jesus' morality or cause, or if it can simply mean a moral person, then of course it is possible to add reincarnation to a "Christian's" religious portfolio.

But if a Christian takes the witness of the New Testament seriously as it pertains to the character, purpose, mission, and demands of Jesus Christ, and if he believes what Jesus taught, then he must reject anything that is antithetical to that teaching. As demonstrated earlier, Jesus taught something radically different from reincarnation. Strictly speaking, one who believes what Jesus taught about life and death cannot with integrity accept the theory of reincarnation.

It is true that a handful of Christian preachers and theologians have argued for the possibility of reincarnation. But I have found that this is usually the result of either a prior rejection of New Testament theology or a failure to use the word *reincarnation* with any care or precision.

Hence, the answer to the question at hand must remain no. This is entirely a matter of logic, not a question of taste or preference.

In the same way that an atheist cannot believe in a personal God and remain an atheist, and a republican cannot remain a republican and believe in the monarchy, so a Christian cannot believe in reincarnation and remain a Christian.

Is it not narrow to insist upon resurrection only? Have not many Christians broadened their ideas and accepted both resurrection and reincarnation?

This question contains many of the same false assumptions as the last question, but it deserves separate treatment, since it embodies other very common misconceptions.

First of all, the notion that ideas can be "narrow" was exploded decades ago by the great British journalist G.K. Chesterton, who pointed out that ideas can never be broader than they are.[4] They can be right or wrong, defended or refuted, soundly based or ill-conceived, but they can never be narrow or broad. Insisting upon resurrection, reincarnation, or any other idea over another metaphysical alternative is not being narrow; rather, it is being convinced that one idea is correct and that its opposite is incorrect. A person's *perspective* can be narrow when he allows a limited number of ideas to enter his consideration either by lack of exposure or by conscious suppression; but this is another matter entirely.

Secondly, some people who consider themselves Christians still manage to incorporate the theory of reincarnation into their belief system. But they have done so not by "broadening" their perspective, but by changing their views. That is to say, they have rejected one doctrine and accepted another doctrine; they have turned away from one idea and embraced another idea. But they have not become more narrow or broad: they have been *converted*. And insofar as the conversion is to belief in reincarnation, the change represents a 180-degree turnabout. To call this a "broadening of perspective" is rather like saying that Henry VIII broadened his perspective on the wedding vows to include more than one wife.

4. G.K. Chesterton, *Orthodoxy* (Garden City, N.Y.: Image, 1959).

DOES NOT THE OLD TESTAMENT TEACH THE DOCTRINE OF KARMA
IN THE COMMANDMENT, "AN EYE FOR AN EYE AND A TOOTH FOR A
TOOTH"?

This is one of the most misunderstood statements in the
Bible. A close study of both Old Testament Scriptures and the legal
structures of the communities around Israel reveals that this was a
common piece of legislation, designed not to ensure vengeance, but
to limit it. It was not intended that the rule always be taken literally,
as can be seen in one application of the law described in Exodus
21:26-27:

> And if a man strikes the eye of his male or female slave, and destroys it,
> he shall let him go free on account of his eye. And if he knocks out a
> tooth of his male or female slave, he shall let him go free on account of
> his tooth.

Even when the rule is applied in a more literal way, the proper
meaning may be paraphrased, "*No more than* an eye for an eye, and *no
more than* a tooth for a tooth." It is not difficult to see why this
limitation was necessary. If one person kills another person's horse,
the second person might in retaliation burn down the other's home;
and so in counter-retaliation the one whose home was burned would
murder the other; and so on. Such is the normal course of human
revenge—an ever escalating series of self-justified attacks and
counterattacks. As it was in biblical times, so it is today.

This biblical injunction is not a mechanical law like karma,
but is a conscious limitation placed upon the uncontrolled passions of
human vengeance.

WHY SHOULD ONE BELIEVE THAT REINCARNATION THEORY IS THE
RESULT OF DEMONIC DECEPTION?

The answer to this question must come from the New
Testament's view of the human situation. Here we are told that,
despite our subjective perceptions of the world, the human race is in
the grip of an awesome evil force, a force so powerful that we are
utterly incapable of extricating ourselves from its grasp. It is as though
we were born into a family or race that for many centuries has been

under the domination of some hostile and malignant ruler.

This view cannot be objected to in principle, because what we know of the world strongly suggests that it could be true. We are all painfully familiar with the frightful excesses of the powerful and the power-hungry. We hear reports of their viciousness with such monotonous frequency that we seldom pay attention. However, when our attention is arrested, we are impressed by one common feature—the use of deception. Every successful tyrant is carefully schooled in the art of duplicity, censorship, and outright lying, for truth rarely serves the ends of slavery.

But what motive would there be for demonic forces to keep the human race in the dark as regards the ultimate issues of life and death? By analogy, we may ask the question, What motive would there be for any tyrant to deceive great numbers of people? The answer is not too hard to find. Deception is necessary to gain and maintain power and advantage over others. Who has not observed this strange phenomenon: A boss maintains power over his employees by the skillful use of a lie; a politician secures advantage over his opponents or constituents by the careful manipulation of the facts; a husband or wife withholds information in order to reduce the other's bargaining position.

We might guess at the motives for gaining power in such mundane cases, but why would any personality want to gain total control of the world and all of its inhabitants?

The question touches upon the central issue of the fallen human heart, namely, our inexplicable compulsion to manipulate everyone and everything around us, to create our own reality; in other words, to play that part that is reserved for God alone, to act out the role of the Creator, to be God Himself. This is the fundamental form of human rebellion and sin. According to the Bible, it was the first act of insurrection against the Creator, promulgated in ages long forgotten by the earliest princes of the heavenly realm in a struggle as ancient as the dawn of creation (see Genesis 3).

Why should this rebellion in the sphere of the spirit draw into its web the human race and the physical realm? This is not hard to answer, for from the point of view of the Bible it is the most predictable result. The human family is the crown of God's creation, the high watermark of His established order, and a primary source of His praise and glory. It is no wonder that any rebellion against the Creator would ultimately focus its attention on the highest order of the created world and the object of the Creator's love and pleasure. If the principal measure of value in the sphere of the spirit is to receive glory, honor, and praise, then what greater treasure could be captured than the being that was designed specifically for the purpose of giving glory, honor, and praise?

All these images of rebellion, deception, and enslavement will seem pure fiction to those who are not even convinced that there are such things as spirits; but this inability to accept spiritual realities comes from the conditioning of a materialistic culture. As soon as a person admits even the possibility of the existence of spirits, he cannot avoid the force of the analogies that are all around us; and thus the door is open for the possibility of tyrants, lords, and even *lunatics* of the spiritual order seeking to enslave all other beings.

What is the specific role played by the doctrine of reincarnation in this drama? It quite clearly dissolves the whole structure of redemption and forgiveness that is presented to the person by the hearing of the gospel of Christ. With its teaching of many lives in which to work out the balance of karma, it constitutes a doctrine of *sin without grace*, of transgression without pardon. It teaches righteousness by works and therefore appeals to that human pride which lies at the heart of sin and alienation from God.

The end result of this is to remove all reason for awaiting a deliverer. Where there is no longing or expectation of a Messiah, he is not recognized or acknowledged when he comes. Jesus Christ then comes to represent in His cross and resurrection no more than an answer for which there is no question. For the reincarnationist, all the life and work of Christ is irrelevant.

BECAUSE NOTHING WAS WRITTEN DURING JESUS' LIFETIME, HOW DO WE KNOW THAT THE NEW TESTAMENT TEACHES WHAT JESUS REALLY TAUGHT?

First, we do not know for certain that nothing was written about Jesus during His lifetime. We know only that what we have preserved for us was not written until after His death and resurrection. It is conceivable that much of Jesus' teaching was written down even as He taught and was preserved in sources that did not survive beyond the first century. In fact, most scholars argue for the view that Semitic sources lie behind the New Testament Greek gospels, and that those sources were probably a combination of both oral and written traditions.

The Jewish people who were the first followers of Jesus believed strongly that the spoken word was more accurate and reliable than the written word. Thus, important traditions were kept alive as long as possible in oral form. By the time of Jesus, the Jews had learned through centuries of training to preserve important teaching orally with startling accuracy. (This is simply a matter of historical fact, and can be shown easily from Jewish histories and secular works dealing with Jewish culture.) The first Christians considered the teaching of Jesus to be that of God Himself, and so treated it in the same way as they had always treated divine revelation.

In any case, it has been discussed that the oral tradition was codified and preserved in writing long before the first witnesses had passed from the scene, and that the texts were open to the corrections of the friendly as well as the hostile people who had heard the words of Jesus and had seen what He had done.

Moreover, it is not true, as it is usually assumed, that the gospels were the earliest writings of the New Testament. The letters of the apostle Paul are considered the earliest, and his letters to the church at Thessalonica appear to be first—probably in the early fifties of the first century, a very short time after the crucifixion. Many scholars detect earlier sources even within Paul's writing, such as hymns, quotations, and creedal forms. If true, this would bring us even closer—at least chronologically—to the original teaching of Jesus.

If it is argued further that the New Testament writers were given to excessive creativity in their representation of the teaching of Jesus, we are in a fortunate position for testing this theory against the documents themselves. If it can be shown that Luke, for example, accurately represents religious, philosophical, and political schools of thought such as the Stoics or Athenians, then we are fairly safe in assuming that he faithfully recorded Jesus' teachings as well. It is a small matter to check Luke's portrait of those other belief systems against the representations of those same groups in secular sources. I refer the reader to some of the fine work already done.[5]

Another more immediately available check may be made by the reader. It is generally believed among scholars that the gospel of Mark was the first of the three synoptic gospels to be completed, and that Matthew and Luke borrowed from Mark in their compositions. Assuming this is true, one may simply compare the gospels of Mark and Luke in their detail and see that although there are some noticeable variations, the teaching of Jesus in Luke is preserved substantially as it existed in Mark.

I encourage the reader to pursue this matter with some energy, for in doing so he will be confronted with a massive body of evidence that will strengthen his confidence in the basic reliability of the New Testament and in the dependability of its writers, who were careful *conservers*, rather than *creators*, of tradition.

WHY DO CHRISTIANS ASSUME THAT RESURRECTION NEED NOT BE PROVED EXCEPT ON THE EVIDENCE OF ONE EXAMPLE? ARE THERE NOT OTHER EXAMPLES OF RESURRECTION THAT HAVE BEEN DOCU-MENTED?

This question is especially intriguing because it reflects one of the greatest misconceptions prevalent among people outside the church. It assumes that resurrection can be argued for simply on the basis of the sheer mass of empirical evidence. It puts the Christian conception of resurrection in the same category with dinosaurs, volcanoes, and meteorites—all of which require the same sort of hard evidence before a reasonable person will believe in them. This is precisely the method employed by proponents of reincarnation; and, insofar as reincarnation can be argued for at all, it is the *only* employable method.

5. C.K. Barrett, *Luke the Historian in Recent Study* (Philadelphia: Fortress, 1970); I.H. Marshall, *Luke: Historian and Theologian* (Grand Rapids: Zondervan, 1970); Leander E. Keck and J.L. Martyn, *Studies in Luke-Acts* (New York: Abingdon, 1966).

As discussed earlier, Christians do not base their belief in resurrection upon a number of resurrections in history. Rather, the entire argument depends on the resurrection of Jesus Christ. If it could be shown somehow that the resurrection of Jesus Christ was a hoax, then there could be no compelling argument in favor of the Christian view of survival.

Moreover, Jesus' resurrection is intrinsically bound up with His character and mission. Some years ago, in a heated debate with one young revolutionary, I was confronted with an opinion that was rather novel to me. That young idealist surprised even his fellows by stating that Jesus Christ did in fact rise from the dead, but that he regarded the event as inconsequential, with no significance beyond itself. It was, in his view, simply a quirk of nature, a freak accident. There was one educated person who had been forced by the weight of historical evidence to admit that the resurrection had happened; yet he rejected Christian faith. In order to maintain his unbelief, he had to select and discard elements of the New Testament arbitrarily, separating Jesus' resurrection from the meaning of Jesus.

This line of reasoning can carry no weight. Christ announced that He was the focal point of God's revelation upon the earth. He performed miracles to demonstrate His God-given power. He claimed authority far beyond what any other human being could claim. He repeatedly promised that He would be killed by the hands of men and brought back to life again on the third day. In view of all this, it is absurd to think that His subsequent resurrection from the dead would have no meaning.

Resurrection is believable to us because Jesus Christ taught it, and because He came back from the dead to vindicate His authority. In the New Testament He has given us more reasons to regard Him as an authority than any other person. For Christians it is enough that He, and He alone, should be the final word on life and death, even if every other human being on earth disagreed with Him.

Some events are so colossal that only one of their kind is required to change history forever. On the desert of New Mexico in July 1945, many of the greatest scientists in the world watched the first detonation of the atom bomb, and they saw that human life could never again be the same. So, too, the disciples of Jesus who witnessed

His resurrection came to realize that this one event was sufficient to change all of life for all time.

HOW CAN CHRISTIANS BELIEVE IN AN ETERNAL HELL?

This surely is one of the major stumbling blocks to faith for many sensitive people. The mere mention of the word *hell* conjures up so many fearful, terrifying images and has been so abused in modern preaching that the whole concept appears patently absurd and is often rejected out of hand. Consequently, those who believe in hell are regarded either as grossly ignorant or cruel and heartless. The word itself is so overlaid with misconceptions that it might be wiser to use some other word or phrase more capable of explanation and clarification. Or, if the word is used at all, it should be rooted firmly in the context of the Bible and should be clearly defined.

Before attempting to define hell, we must face the question, By what authority do you believe in it? If it can be established that the doctrine comes to us by strong authority, then we can busy ourselves in finding out what its nature and characteristics are. The church's answer has been simply, "Jesus taught it." That has been enough. If Jesus has been proved trustworthy to teach on matters of life and death, then it is sufficient that it comes to us on His authority.

It is surprising how many people contest the assertion that Jesus taught this doctrine. What seems self-evident upon an even casual reading of the gospels is almost universally challenged. "Prove to me that Jesus taught hell!" is, in my experience, a common demand, and I know of no other answer than, "Read the gospels."

I suppose people think that one so loving and kind as Jesus could never have taught something as terrible and cruel as hell; and so it must have come from some vengeful Christian who secretly changed the Bible. However, in simply reading the gospels through it becomes evident that Jesus taught the doctrine even more aggressively than anyone else, and that it is integral to His teaching on many other subjects. Even His quotes and allusions from the Old Testament concentrate largely upon those portions of Psalms and Deuteronomy that contain strong messages of judgment and separation. The note of judgment so thoroughly permeates His teaching that to remove it is to render much of His message nonsensical. If the gospels preserve anything for us of the teaching of Jesus, then it may be safely concluded that Jesus had as a leading motif the doctrine of separation from God caused by rebellion against Him.

However, the exact nature of hell is not self-evident in Jesus' teachings. In a recent public debate at a local college, I was chided by my opponent for trying to "have one's history both ways": that is, for believing in a doctrine of hell but shying away from the literal picture of flames and torture (as is depicted, for example, in Dante's *Inferno*). It seemed hypocritical to him that I should maintain the doctrine but deny what he believed to be the Bible's clear representation of hell, a fiery inferno with all manner of horrific furniture.

Without belaboring this point, I will say that a hell with or without flames is still essentially hell—that is, separation from the love, care, and purpose of the eternal God. And a hell without flames is no nicer than one with flames, since the worst possible end from the Bible's point of view is to be outside the presence of God. The New Testament uses the language of the Old Testament, including the imagery of fire, to communicate how thoroughly God will destroy that which is stubbornly opposed to Him. Fire is simply the symbol best suited to the Bible's purpose here.

The inadvisability of interpreting "fire" literally in the Old Testament may be seen in this description of how God answered David's prayer for deliverance:

> Then the earth shook and quaked;
> And the foundations of the mountains were trembling
> And were shaken, because He was angry.
> Smoke went up out of His nostrils,
> And fire from His mouth devoured;
> Coals were kindled by it.
>   (Psalm 18:7-8)

The historical setting for this passage is found in 2 Samuel 21 and 22. Here it is clear that literal fire was not present in the destruction of David's enemies; rather, "fire" was the linguistic tool used to depict the surety of God's judgment.

Moreover, if the literalness of this symbol in Jesus' teaching is

pressed, then how can Jesus' references to hell as "outer darkness" be
explained? (Matthew 8:12; 22:13; 25:30).

Quibbling over the details of the New Testament metaphors
for hell in order to make it either more or less terrifying is to miss the
point. The imagery is clear enough (cf. Mark 9:43-48; Luke 16:19-31)
to justify our worst fears of it; and such fear should drive one to the
mercy and grace of God.

Clearly, the reason Jesus gave us warnings about hell was not
to present a literal picture of the place, but to show us the staggering
consequences of being cast out of the Creator's commonwealth and
exiled from our intended home. God does not send people to hell
because they are unchurched; hell is where people insist on going
when they refuse heaven. God does not force people to go to hell; it is
just that He does not force them into heaven. Like a grieving parent,
He says to those of us who choose hell, "Thy will be done."[6]

IT IS NOT FAIR THAT PEOPLE WHO HAVE NEVER HEARD THE NAME
OF CHRIST SHOULD BE JUDGED BY HIM. WOULD NOT REINCARNA-
TION PROVIDE A SECOND CHANCE FOR THEM?

It is true that reincarnation, if valid, could provide an
opportunity for those who have never heard the gospel of Christ to
hear it. This view has a certain amount of appeal, for it seems to
relieve some of the apparent tension between the biblical statements
that Christ is the only way to God and that God is a just God.
However, the reincarnationist answer creates more problems than it
solves.

First, we have already seen that substantial evidence is
lacking for the theory of reincarnation. It really does not matter what
questions it answers if it is not true. No amount of practical
application can justify a belief for which there is no convincing
evidence.

Second, for the Christian the answer depends on what the
Scriptures teach on the subject, since they are the only reliable
foundation of doctrine for the church. Admittedly, the Bible says
little directly on this subject. Because of the nature and purpose of

6. C.S. Lewis, *Mere Christianity* (Glasgow: William Collins Sons & Co., 1982).

the New Testament, we know more about what happens to those people who consciously, stubbornly refuse the gift of salvation than we do about those who never have heard the gospel. However, we should not despair; a number of key passages in Scripture testify to God's care for all the peoples of the earth.

The Old Testament is riddled with references that bear upon this subject. In many passages (such as Genesis 12:3; 18:18; Psalms 57:9; 96:3; 108:3; Isaiah 45:23; and 61:6, 9) we see that from the beginning God's concern was for all nations and all individuals. Even the election of the Jewish nation was to build them into an instrument by which the knowledge of God would be proclaimed throughout the earth. They were chosen not to be the exclusive beneficiaries of the gifts of God, but to be the *bearers* of those gifts. This was not in fact what happened historically, but according to the writers of the Old Testament it was the clear intention of God; and Scripture makes it clear that God was angry when the commission was not fulfilled.

This theme, so firmly rooted in the Old Testament, is confirmed in the preaching of Jesus (for example, Matthew 24:14; 28:19; Mark 13:10; Luke 24:47). It is further developed by the apostle Paul (Romans 3:29; Galatians 2:2; Ephesians 3:6; Colossians 1:27), who was regarded as the chief missionary to the Gentiles. Thus, there can be no question that God's intention is, and always was, to make Himself available to the world, and that He wants the knowledge of Himself to be proclaimed by His people to every living creature.

It is obvious that neither Israel nor the church has fulfilled its commission, and that millions of human beings have passed through this life without ever hearing the name of Jesus Christ. But in view of all that we know from Scripture about God's love for all those people, it is not unreasonable to assume that His plan of redemption in some way touches upon them.

The writings of Luke give us some indication as to how one may view this matter. In the book of Acts, from time to time in the narrative we meet "worshipers of God." These were neither Jew nor Christian, but seemingly knew enough of God to attempt to worship Him in some way. We do not know what their creeds were, nor can we say how much about God they actually knew; we deduce only that they understood *something* about Him and therefore worshiped Him. The centurion Cornelius (Acts 10:1) and Lydia of Thyatira (Acts 16:14) were both called "worshipers of God," and the Spit of God led the apostles specifically to them at the starting points of particular evangelistic outreaches.

One may infer from this that God has plans and strategies for making the gospel known to the single, obscure person in the backwaters of the world who is responsive to the many and hidden ways He uses to communicate with His creatures.

The New Testament anticipates the argument that, since some people are conditioned by their cultures or backgrounds to seek God and some are not, it would be unfair to judge those who are not so conditioned. It was undoubtedly the view of Jesus, and was more systematically expressed in the writings of the apostle Paul, that each person in the world is responsible before God, regardless of background or station in life. In Romans 1 and 2, we see that this is because all men, by virtue of being God's creatures, have some innate knowledge of the Creator. So it is that everyone stands culpable before God.

The history of missions abounds with examples of how the most unreached peoples on earth have exhibited profound awareness of the God who in the New Testament is intimately described and revealed through Jesus Christ.

Whereas we do not know what His Spirit is doing among those outside the reach of the missionary, we do know that He deals with them in kindness and justice (Psalm 145:17). As one sensitive pastor said in reference to the unknown peoples of the earth, "Last seen in the hands of God." Yet even with this confidence in His justice, the church ever stands strictly under Christ's injunction to "Go therefore and make disciples of all the nations . . . " (Matthew 28:19).

SINCE ALL RELIGIONS ARE FUNDAMENTALLY THE SAME, WHY CAN'T THERE BE MANY WAYS TO SALVATION AND IMMORTALITY?

Much of the answer to this has been given in the sections

describing the uniqueness of Jesus Christ and the import of His resurrection as a verification of His teaching. However, because some of the hidden assumptions of the question have not been addressed, it shall be treated briefly.

There are two false notions behind this question: (1) that all religious systems are basically the same, their differences being superficial; and (2) that the "equality of all religions" approach is an affirmation of all religions.

(1) The study of beliefs about the afterlife clearly shows that religions are *not* essentially the same. The truth is exactly the opposite. Whereas the "furniture" of different systems has many surface similarities (i.e., sacred writings, priests, rituals, etc.), the cores of the religions of the world are fundamentally different from one another.

So we see that both reincarnational religions and Christianity hold that the human race will some day be in some way restored. But "restoration" for one is its exact opposite for the other. In reincarnational thought, life in the body on earth means estrangement, and restoration means reaching a resting place of nonmaterial existence. The Bible presents the inversion of this view: since the created, physical order is the handiwork of God, it is a mark of disorder to have the body separated from the immaterial part of the human creation. Restoration, then, in the theology of the Bible, is a reinstatement of the created order of things as it was originally intended to be, at an even higher, transformed level.

(2) The cozy conviction that all faiths lead to the same happy end is not what it appears to be. Seeming to be a positive appraisal of all religions, it is actually a *denial* of all religions.

Consider this question: Who of the followers of any given religion benefit from it? There are only two possible answers: either only those who sincerely follow the precepts of the religion, or everyone who identifies with the religion, however loosely.

Now, if only the faithful reach salvation, then we are faced with the difficult task of finding them. Anyone who has studied world religions is aware of the chasm between what people believe and what they do, and that painfully few actually lead their lives in accordance with the tenets and ordinances of the faith they profess. We are left with a small minority of people who have the time and the inclination to "keep the faith," and who achieve the desired goal.

But in saying that only a few reach salvation, we are back to the same problem that is faced by those who dislike the exclusive claims of Christianity.

The only other alternative is to say that not only the faithful reach salvation, but also the unfaithful, the nominal, the hypocritical.

But if the hypocrite or the insincere can attain the rewards of a particular religion, then there is really no need at all for the convoluted doctrines, mysterious rituals, and stringent practices of *any* religion. If all religions are ultimately unnecessary to securing anything for their followers—if salvation is automatic—then the original proposition is not an affirmation of that religion but is instead its denial.

To argue for the equality of all religions, then, is either to deny the integrity of all religions or to affirm that salvation is only for the few; thus, the reason for making the statement is destroyed. We have come full circle, and we have gone nowhere.

SINCE CHRISTIANS REJECT THE IDEA OF KARMA, HOW CAN THEY EXPLAIN THAT ONE CHILD CAN BE BORN RICH, ONE POOR, ONE DEFORMED OR RETARDED, ONE HEALTHY, ONE DEAD AT BIRTH? HOW CAN THIS BE FAIR?

This is another way of asking the perennial question regarding human suffering in general. It is frequently thought that the two Christian tenets "God is loving and just" and "God is omnipotent" create in the face of human experience a tension so great as to be unresolvable. For if God is loving and just, then how could He stand by and let what happens in the world continue? This concern is often so powerful as to keep people from faith in the God of Scripture. The difficulty goes even beyond the issue of deformed children, poverty, early death, and so forth and leads us headlong into the problem of the human condition.

Before attempting to answer the question, I must first restate an earlier point: although it is correct that reincarnation theory, if true, would offer us an explanation for this problem (for example, a deformed child in this view is simply paying his debt from a past life), this is not a compelling reason to accept the theory. Many nihilists, agnostics, and atheists use the same evidence to support the view that the universe and human life have no meaning or purpose whatever. Clearly then, just because the theory presumes to give an explanation for one of the mysteries of life is no sign that it is the truth.

Christian theology offers a coherent response to the age-old question of suffering. There are three preliminary observations that we must make before we can start to answer the question.

First, the question of suffering and God's apparent lack of response to it can most honestly be asked by one who is consciously doing everything he can to obey the will of God and to turn from his own sin. The reason for this is very clear. If a person is not actively involved in attempting to do the will of God in the world, then his cry against suffering, pain, or injustice rings hollow. For he is saying in effect, "I insist that God step in *over there* and stop that suffering and injustice; but I want none of God's interference when it comes to my own life."

This person demands that God intervene everywhere in the world to put a halt to pain and suffering except at that point where he himself is causing it. He thinks God must stop his neighbor from committing crimes against others, but He must not interfere with his own lying, cheating, or defrauding. He thinks that God should have prevented the Nazi concentration camps, but not that He should prevent his own private anti-Semitism. This is to say that He should be tolerant of humanity's sin and idolatry, but intolerant of any suffering that is a consequence of it. This exactly is the rebel's position; were he to see it for what it is, he might temper his anger at God.

Second, when considering the question of suffering we should not concentrate on sensational incidents in lands far away while ignoring our own neighborhood. It is easy to ask how God can allow people in Chile to die in an earthquake while neglecting to consider that even more people die every day in wealthy countries of cancer and auto accidents. We really know very little about who is suffering most in the world. To the list of earthquakes, pestilence, flood, famine, cancer, and accidents we must also consider psycho-logical suffering in all of its varied manifestations. Suffering and pain are the lot of the entire human race, and we must keep that in mind while framing our questions. This is not to say that suffering is everywhere *equal*, but that it is *universal*.

While in the hospital for minor surgery a few years ago, I was placed in a room with a man dying of cancer. I heard this man cry out in pain day and night as the cancer slowly consumed his inner organs. He pleaded constantly for more painkiller. I thought at the time that it would have been hard to find anyone on the earth who was suffering more than this man. The earthquake victim, the peasant being washed away in the flood, the political prisoner being tortured; which one of them could have persuaded this man that he was better off—in one of the finest hospitals in the world, in one of the most affluent areas of the country? If the question of suffering is asked anywhere, surely it must be asked everywhere.

A third factor to consider is the biblical view of history, without which the question of suffering and evil cannot adequately be answered or even asked. Here we find things that are very difficult for the modern person to accept, because they contradict the most dearly held tenets of contemporary mentality.

It is my understanding that the Bible sees human life as a war, a total and all-consuming war with enormous forces of evil operating everywhere and in every person. Some theologians describe our era as being between two great events, the turning point of the war and the end of the war, similar to the time between D-Day (the decisive battle in Europe in the Second World War) and V-E Day (the final victory in Europe in 1945). The all-important turning point of this cosmic war against evil came when Jesus Christ fought and won on the cross. All that remains for us is a "clean-up operation," where ultimate victory for the believer is already assured. But even though the war is already determined to be won by Christ and His kingdom, many injuries are yet to be inflicted. This means that we are still subject to all the invading forces of death and disintegration; our bodies are dying, our world is fading, the present age is passing away.

Anything less than this image of total war cannot provide an adequate interpretation for the stupendous force of suffering and terror in the world. Any attempt philosophically to underplay the full blast of these realities must ring hollow in our ears.

We can now return to the original question and give some answers, keeping the above principles in mind.

It is fair to say that a great many examples of the problem can be accounted for simply on the basis of human sin and stubbornness. If a child is born in dire poverty, it is because the mass of human beings who allowed the situation of poverty to go unchallenged have neither the desire nor the compassion to change the situation. This callousness was one of the central themes in the preaching of the Old Testament prophets. They railed against people who nonchalantly stood by, thereby perpetuating the evil system of exploitation that produced poverty in the midst of plenty. (It is noteworthy that the clearest explanation in the Bible for the destruction of Sodom, Genesis 19:1-29, is that the people had plenty of everything and did not care for the poor and needy, Ezekiel 16:49.) Some have counted over 800 biblical references to God's concern for basic justice.

For example, the responsibility for some cases of child deformation may be laid at the feet of parents—the mother who abused her body in some way with various drugs or failed to carry out normal precautions when pregnant, the father who physically abused the mother, and so on. Whereas God frequently rescues us from our foolishness and ignorance, He just as often allows us to see the results of our errors and uses them to bring about His purposes.

To the objection that human suffering is not fair, the biblical response is that the unfairness is not so much toward the created being as it is toward the Creator, who made a perfect world that through its own willful rebellion went astray. What is clear from Scripture is that the whole universe (including the human population, the animal, plant, and mineral kingdoms), is in a radical state of deformation. That which was once created perfect and good is now in a fallen condition because of human rebellion against the Creator, and a deformed child is only one evidence of the more fundamental problem that touches the entire race.

It is one of the cornerstones of Christian theology that God has come to us in the very locus of our sin and suffering. Jesus of Nazareth, born into grinding poverty in the midst of political oppression, infanticide, and cruelty on every hand, reveals to us the fullest expression of God the Creator. He lived a life without sin and was tortured and killed by cowards in the most ignominious way known at the time. God chose to bring about that event that would become the turning point of human history, the death and resurrection of Jesus Christ, and to cause it to occur in the very midst of the worst that humanity could do.

Thus, humanity's darkest hour was the stage upon which was acted out the redemption of the race. Our unfairness and injustice became in the hands of God the raw material for building our eternal home. It was as if God was saying to us, "You may do your worst, but I shall use your worst as the focal point of My victory in bringing you back to Me. This shall be done in such a way that you can have no credit for yourselves in the process."

It is this assurance that God is with us even in our rebellion against Him, and is absorbing the rebellion's consequences in Himself, which has been the comfort of believers for centuries. God has been disclosed to us not as a divine narcissist who admires His own glory in the heavens, but as the near and present Friend, who comes to us and suffers with us and in so doing wins us back to Himself.

DOES NOT NATURE, WITH ITS CYCLICAL MOVEMENT OF SEASONS, TESTIFY MORE TO REINCARNATION THAN TO RESURRECTION?

It is a common view among reincarnationists that the repetitive change of seasons is indirect testimony for the theory of reincarnation. This seems perfectly logical. The ongoing cycle of new life followed by aging, disintegration and death, renewal of life, and so on seems to speak of a cyclical rather than linear movement of history.

One should not be too quickly persuaded by this, however. Nature has always been a poor indicator of ultimate realities, as a brief look at the history of philosophy and theology can show. Nature is simply too ambiguous to be of much use in these matters. For every person who can look at nature and see beauty, love, and order, another can point to as much evidence of cruelty, ugliness, and caprice. It is all too easy for a purely subjective view of life to creep in when trying to deduce ultimate meaning from what is around us in creation—especially when we live in what the Bible describes as a "fallen" and disordered cosmos.

And nature's support for reincarnation is disappointing in the end. The physical sciences depict the universe as an ongoing, constantly regenerating system where life climbs ever upward, but which eventually winds down, cools off, or burns out. The universe as we know it is dying, and no amount of sentiment or optimism can change this known fact. From our very limited point of view we see an alternating, pendulum-like movement from life to death, a carousel that seems as if it will spin forever, always moving in perfectly predictable sequences. But like the carousel, the universe must one day come to a full stop, as both the physical sciences and the Bible will attest.

Therefore, if nature tells us anything, it tells us that we are locked into a process of death; in the end, she offers no hope for survival. Whatever cycles within cycles we may observe in life, all cycles are destined to end.

Much of this, of course, a reincarnationist would not necessarily deny. But this agreement does not amount to anything very substantial. For the Christian believer, nature cannot be seen as an interpreter of ultimate reality; rather, ultimate reality—God— must be the interpreter of nature. And this is precisely what occurs in the Bible.

History in the Bible is always "salvation history," and unless one brings this key to the study of it, only ambiguity emerges. When history is studied within the framework of "salvation history," one finds that the seasons begin to play an intriguing role in its interpretation. God's interventions in history, His principal acts of deliverance, often occur in the *springtime*. God seems to reserve the most important moments of His deliverance for that time of the year when life, color, beauty, and warmth surge out of the earth almost as a surprise after a bleak and bitter winter.

If indeed God is speaking to us through the seasons, then we should understand that the last season is not winter but spring. The last moment of human history and destiny is not winter's grave but springtime's explosion of new life. In this sense, the seasons have stamped upon them the mark of resurrection—not the nothingness of nonbodily existence, but the fullness and glory of new creations no longer susceptible to disintegration and death. Nature does not speak of reincarnation but of resurrection.

And this truth comes to us on the basis of authority, namely, the authority of one person, Jesus Christ. It is He who causes us to believe that the last season is springtime. Otherwise, we are lost in a cycle of living and dying through innumerable seasons; eternal time wanderers locked into a metaphysical shell game, in search of non-bodily, nonpersonal nonexistence. It is in one Man that we hear the message that there was a beginning and there shall be an end, that there is one life, one death, one resurrection, and one judgment.

Glossary

DEMONIC   The realm of evil spirits. In Christian theology, the host of created spirit-beings who are in rebellion against the Creator.

HUMANISM   In philosophy, a system of thought that holds to the primacy of man rather than to any abstract or metaphysical system. This view holds that man is the measure of all things, and in our time it has become virtually a religion in itself.

HYPNOTIC REGRESSION   The achievement of retrocognition ("past life memories") through hypnosis.

IMMORTALITY OF THE SOUL   A philosophical and religious belief that affirms the inherent indestructibility of the essence of the human being, the soul. This view is in contrast to the Christian doctrine of immortality, which holds that God alone sustains existence.

MATERIALISM   In philosophy, the belief that all reality is essentially reducible to the material world, thus excluding the immaterial realm of spirits. In its practical outworking it often leads to a preoccupation with material goods.

METEMPSYCHOSIS   The ancient Greek term meaning functionally the same thing as reincarnation.

MONISM   The notion that all reality may be reduced to a single, unifying principle. Hinduism affirms that the nonmaterial world is the ultimate reality, whereas materialism affirms the same for the world of matter.

NATURALISM The view that asserts there is nothing real beyond nature. Human beings are therefore understood strictly in terms of environment and heredity.

PARAPSYCHOLOGY The scientific study of phenomena not fully explainable by conventional principles of psychology or science.

PAST LIFE THERAPY The treatment of psychological disturbances that presupposes that present conflicts and problems are the result of one's past life.

PREEXISTENCE OF SOULS The belief that every soul possesses a life and experience before incarnation.

RETROCOGNITION The knowledge—some would say "memories"—of the past, achieved through paranormal means.

TRANSMIGRATION OF SOULS The movement of the soul after death from one bodily form to another.

Bibliography

Albrecht, Mark. *Reincarnation: A Christian Appraisal.* Downers Grove, Ill.: InterVarsity, 1982.

Barrett, C.K. *Luke the Historian in Recent Study.* Philadelphia: Fortress, 1970.

Browning, Norma Lee. *The Psychic World of Peter Hurkos.* Garden City, N.Y.: Doubleday, 1970.

Bruce, F.F. *The New Testament Documents: Are They Reliable?* Grand Rapids: Eerdmans, 1968.

Chesterton, G.K. *Orthodoxy.* Garden City, N.Y.: Image, 1959.

Gallup, George, Jr., and Procter, William. *Adventures in Immortality.* New York: McGraw-Hill, 1982.

Head, Joseph, and Cranston, S.L. *Reincarnation: The Phoenix Fire Mystery.* New York: Warner, 1977.

Hurkos, Peter. *Psychic.* Indianapolis: Bobbs-Merrill, 1961.

Keck, Leander E., and Martyn, J.L. *Studies in Luke-Acts.* New York: Abingdon, 1966.

Lewis, C.S. *Mere Christianity.* Glasgow: William Collins Sons & Co., 1982.

Marshall, I.H. *Luke: Historian and Theologian.* Grand Rapids: Zondervan, 1970.

Montgomery, John Warwick. *History and Christianity.* Downers Grove, Ill.: InterVarsity, 1965.

Moody, Raymond A. *Life After Life.* New York: Bantam, 1975.

Niebuhr, Reinhold. *The Nature and Destiny of Man,* vol. 1. New York: Scribner's, 1964.

Puharich, Andrijah. *Beyond Death's Door.* Nashville: Thomas Nelson, 1978.

Robinson, John A.T. *Can We Trust the New Testament?* Grand Rapids, Eerdmans, 1977.

Steiger, Brad. *You Will Live Again.* New York: Dell, 1978.

Stevenson, Ian. *Twenty Cases Suggestive of Reincarnation.* New York: American Society for Psychical Research, 1966.

Strack, H.L., and Billerbeck, P. *Kommentar zum Neuen Testament aus Talmud und Midrasch,* vol. 2. Munich: Beck, 1974.

Thomas, P.J. *Hindu Religion, Customs and Manners.* Bombay: D.B. Taraporevala, Sons & Co., Ltd., 1950.

Moody Press, a ministry of the Moody Bible Institute, is designed for education, evangelization, and edification. If we may assist you in knowing more about Christ and the Christian life, please write us without obligation: Moody Press, c/o MLM, Chicago, Illinois 60610